C000195781

Celebrating the Seasons of Life: Beltane to Mabon

Lore, Rituals, Activities, and Symbols

By

Ashleen O'Gaea

NEW PAGE BOOKS
A division of The Career Press, Inc.
Franklin Lakes, NJ

Copyright © 2005 by Ashleen O'Gaea

All rights reserved under the Pan-American and International Copyright Conventions. This book may not be reproduced, in whole or in part, in any form or by any means electronic or mechanical, including photocopying, recording, or by any information storage and retrieval system now known or hereafter invented, without written permission from the publisher, The Career Press.

CELEBRATING THE SEASONS OF LIFE: BELTANE TO MABON
EDITED BY GINA M. CHESELKA
TYPESET BY EILEEN DOW MUNSON
Cover Illustration and Design by Jean William Naumann
Printed in the U.S.A. by Book-mart Press

To order this title, please call toll-free 1-800-CAREER-1 (NJ and Canada: 201-848-0310) to order using VISA or MasterCard, or for further information on books from Career Press.

The Career Press, Inc., 3 Tice Road, PO Box 687,
Franklin Lakes, NJ 07417
www.careerpress.com
www.newpagebooks.com

Library of Congress Cataloging-in-Publication Data

O'Gaea, Ashleen.
    Celebrating the seasons of life: Beltane to Mabon : lore, rituals, activities, and symbols / by Ashleen O'Gaea.
        p. cm.
    Includes bibliographical references and index.
    ISBN 1-56414-732-0 (pbk.)
        1. Sabbat. 2. Neopaganism--Rituals. 3. Religious calendars--Neopaganism. 4. Witchcraft. I. Title.

BF1572.S28O38 2005
299'.94--dc22

                                                                    2004048621

To Canyondancer,
with whom I hope to celebrate many
more seasons;
and to Hearth's Gate Coven and its
bright future.

I am grateful to the ever-turning Wheel,
  and of course to the Gods, but don't presume They'll read this.
I do hope that the people I'd like to thank will see my gratitude
here, though:

  the recently disbanded Campsight Coven,

  the newly formed Hearth's Gate Coven,

  and the past and present members of the Camping
  Contingent for their cooperation, contributions, and
  inspirations;

  Rick Johnson, Gamlinginn, and Kirk Thomas for sharing
  their experience and offering their information and advice;

  and Canyondancer for his supportive editing.

ontents

reface

When we say "celebrating the seasons of life," what do we mean? Why do we conduct rituals at the Solstices, Equinoxes, and at the other four Sabbats we call "cross-Quarters"? Whether or not we cast our Circles or make any other notice of those days, the Earth will continue to orbit the Sun. Whatever we do, each of us will age and die, succeeded by our children and theirs. So our point is...?

Scientists are finding more and more evidence that our sense of connection to the Earth—to the planet and everything that shares it with us—is "hardwired," along with our notion that all of this is holy. We've evolved as social creatures, and it's our nature to hold kinship holy, whether it's our kinship with each other, with other species, or with the systems and cycles of life itself.

Our word *celebrate* comes from the Latin word *celebratus*, which means "to frequent, go in great numbers, honor." According to my old *Webster's New World Dictionary* (published in 1960 and left over from my husband's undergrad days), modern meanings include "to perform a ritual publicly and solemnly; to commemorate an anniversary, holiday, etc., with ceremony or festivity; to proclaim; and to honor or praise publicly."

While solitary practice of Wicca is valid and most Wiccan Sabbats are observed on a fairly small scale in some covens, we do occasionally celebrate in great numbers—which is great fun. So it is pretty easily understood how celebrating the seasons of life, as marked by Wiccan Sabbats, is both a time for commemorative ritual *and* festivity. It's also easy to recognize the Sabbats as an occasion to publicly honor and praise our Goddess and God. It's more difficult, on the other hand, to understand celebrating the Sabbats in terms of "proclaiming" and "frequenting."

When, historically and in our lore, everybody was Pagan, we did tend to "frequent" certain holy locations. Even if there was no ritual scheduled, individuals passing a well, a spring, or a grove left tokens of reverence, or they simply made an offering of the extra effort it took to climb a holy hill. Stopping to make a votive offering or empower a charm was really quite common.

Our modern understanding of the nature of deity and how magic works is different now than it was in the days of our lore. What was "common knowledge" or cutting-edge theory a millennium ago is, at best, archaic now; at worst, superstitious. What we do share with medieval and older Pagans, real and storied, and with our Neolithic cultural ancestors, too, is a faith that we're part of Nature—that we belong to the Earth's powerful systems and cycles.

We don't respond to those systems and cycles the same way our ancestors did. Most of us don't believe in *Fantasia*-like Greek gods who live on a literal Olympus, or in fairy palaces beneath Britain's megalithic mounds that show up in photographs. The life of the Otherworld is in a different dimension, not in some inaccessible physical location. From our perspective, that dimension can be called metaphorical or subconscious.

This is not the least bit disrespectful, for we also understand that the effect of metaphor, of dreams and emotional experience, show up on CT scans, looking just like the traces of our physical experience. Few of us fall to our knees to beg for mercy when thunder booms and lightning cracks. Few of us expect to meet a triple goddess or a stag-headed god on the street—such an experience is limited to movies and guided meditations.

Movies and guided meditations are definitely among our inspirations, though. *The Lord of the Rings* movies are meaningful to me beyond my attraction to Viggo Mortenson and Orlando Bloom! Gandalf and the hobbit quartet are real to me in ways that my toaster never will be. Then again, Wiccans meet the Goddess and God in other people, every day.

The regal aspects we ascribe to the Gods in our liturgies are marks of the awe and respect we feel for the miraculous nature of the mundane world, which isn't really "mundane" at all when you look closely. Nature and all its workings is the Gods's true nature. From an infant's eyelashes to mountain storms, the power, the diversity, and the synchronicity of Nature is what Wicca holds holy. It's what we seek to name when we speak of the Goddess and God, and when we try to understand Their many aspects in our humble human terms.

Most of us pause to appreciate the magnificent beauty of a gathering storm even if we anticipate the lightning knocking out our power. Even if we're inconveniently snowed in, don't most of us love—at least for a moment—the beauty of the snow as it falls and the diamond-like glitter of the flakes covering the ground? Whether we're inside by a fire or outside about to get soaked to the bone, most of us can smell the rain coming and enjoy both the knowing and the scent.

The smell of freshly mown grass drifting from next door or blocks away perks up our souls. The experience of morning's light glancing through stems, branches, or lampposts alerts us to an imminent Lammas. There's something in the air where you live that lets you know, even if you can't put your finger on it, that it's nigh unto Mabon.

Some of us do manage to find our way to the holy sites in Wicca's homelands—to Newgrange in Ireland, to Stonehenge or Avebury in England, to the Highlands of Scotland, or to the Arthurian coast of Wales. Most of us never get to make those trips, homebound by various circumstances of obligation or finance. Yet we're all followers of a Nature Religion—so instead of frequenting places, we frequent times: our Sabbats.

Several times a day, many of us pass an inconspicuous altar in our homes—a place of offering that others don't recognize, and so can't desecrate. We can all "frequent" our holies in our hearts even if we can't frequent them in the landscape. And sometimes we can be ritual-reverent in nonritual situations. These can be for us as holy as a Circle.

I think more Wiccans today frequent holy places in their thoughts and in their attitudes rather than in person. Though some of us are fortunate enough to live on wide tracts of land or to camp often and so experience the wilder natural powers, we can all feel those influences even when we can't get out to natural shrine-sites. Wonderfully, we all have the power (the ability and the obligation) to make wherever we are and whatever we're doing holy.

Quite literally, we make proclamations of life's seasons in the words and gestures of our Sabbat celebrations, yet these are only echoes of the proclamations life makes of its own seasons. To the attentive, the natural proclamations of the seasons, no matter how subtle, are as clear as a baby's cry. We speak of Sabbats turning the Wheel as we speak of the

Sun going 'round the Earth. In fact, the Earth orbits the Sun, and, in fact, the Sabbats are our joyous response to the clarion calls of Nature—of our Goddess and Her Consort as They dance through our lives.

The dictionary says that the word *celebrate* means "to honor." It is indeed our honor to participate in the cycles of life, which Wiccans call the Spiral Dance. Our celebration of the seasons of life, marked on the Wheel of the Year as Sabbats, honors our Gods and the seasons of Their lives too: His rebirth, growth, and redeath; Her phases as Maiden, Mother, and Crone. Every Sabbat celebrates an anniversary of a step in the Spiral Dance. Every Sabbat is a reminder that we frequent life with every breath.

For a long time it's been hard to celebrate properly. The *public* aspect was missing for hundreds of years, rediscovered but hardly dared by a few families here and there throughout the centuries. It's not entirely restored yet, and not all Wiccans think it should be. (The Druids do, and they're working hard and are achieving some success in bringing public worship back to Neo-Paganism.) But with every turn of the Wheel, with every death and rebirth of the solar year, more and more people understand more and more about Wicca.

It becomes clearer with every Sabbat that the Goddess and God are not locked in antagonistic competition for our souls, but that They share in the loving nurture of life. It becomes clearer to the public that without being afraid of the dark, Neo-Pagan religions are joyous and life-affirming. With the publication of a book such as this and its companion, *Celebrating the Seasons of Life: Samhain to Ostara*, and also by the courage of those who bring what they read here out of the broom closet, Wiccan rites become closer to being true celebrations: public expressions of the honor it is to experience the seasons of life—in these pages, from Beltane to Mabon.

Introduction

You will have noticed that most calendars divide the year into months, and the months are divided into neat little boxes of days. This format tells us that time is linear. Maybe we accept this because the illustrations on most calendars are often so pretty. We have a tendency to forget that the past has anything to do with the present or the future.

Wicca's calendar, the Wheel of the Year, is different. Wicca's calendar is round, reflecting our understanding that time and life are not linear, but cyclical. As a round table allows everyone seated to see each other and keeps anyone's position from being more important than somebody else's, Wicca's round calendar lets the Sabbats "see each other" and keeps them all of equal status.

Well, almost. Traditionally, Samhain and Beltane are the two "most important" Sabbats on Wicca's liturgical calendar. This is because Samhain (pronounced *saw-win*) and Beltane mark the beginnings of the two oldest seasons: Winter and Summer—the two halves of the year. It's out of respect for the "old days" that this book and its sister volume each open with a look at Beltane and Samhain, respectively. In Wiccan terms, the Veil Between the Worlds is thinnest at these Sabbats: It's easier to reconnect with our beloved dead at Samhain (also known as Halloween) and with the fairies at Beltane (which non-Pagans know and love as May Day).

Because they open the two halves of the year, some Wiccan Traditions celebrate Samhain and Beltane more elaborately than they do the other Sabbats. Samhain, for example, is a time for requiems, even if other services have been held for the dead. Beltane, for example, is a favorite Sabbat for *handfastings*, or Wiccan weddings—religious or legal. My former coven, Campsight, always celebrated a little more lavishly at Samhain and Beltane, even though our coven anniversary was at Bride!

(It's also true that Maypole preparations *do* take more time and effort than getting ready for most other Sabbats.)

In these two books, therefore, you'll see a slight favoring of these two Sabbats reflected—but only a little, for the other Sabbats are deeply meaningful on their own, sometimes in more subtle ways. They certainly deserve our attention, and celebration, as much as the two that begin the oldest seasons.

This book and its sister (*Celebrating the Seasons of Life: Samhain to Ostara*) explore each Sabbat thoroughly enough to bring its meaning home to modern Wiccans. These books group the Sabbats around the old division of the Year, which comes from a time when our ancestors were still caring for their herds on the hillsides, so that we can make better sense of the details added since then.

Summer begins at Beltane, and Litha (pronounced *lee-ha*) is mid-Summer despite the fact that most secular calendars say that Summer begins on June 21! Lammas, on August 1, is the beginning of Autumn, and Mabon (the Autumn Equinox) is mid-Autumn no matter what the ordinary calendars say about September 21 (or so). On the Wheel of the Year, they're all Summer holidays. When we understand this, we get a new perspective of both Summer and Autumn. It also helps us remember that Summer does become Autumn, which becomes Winter, which becomes Spring—which makes it clear that time is cyclical. Seasons flow from one another, rolling through the years, dancing the Spiral Dance of Life right along with us.

The Wheel of the Year actually combines two calendars: the agricultural and the astronomical. (That's astronomical, *not* astrological. Many Wiccans are interested in astrology, but it's not "part of" Wicca.) The agricultural year is concerned with when to plant and harvest and when to move domestic herds from the pastures to barns. The astronomical calendar has to do with tides and seasons, which depend on the relative position of the Earth to the Sun and Moon. (This is why the dates of the Solstices and Equinoxes vary by a few days every year. Some Wiccans standardize the dates as the 21st day of each Solstice and Equinox month, while others follow the changing dates. Still others—and this is legitimate too—keep the feasts on the nearest weekend.)

In the old days of our lore, people who kept farms and tended animals were only casually aware of Solstices and Equinoxes. Their attention was on the change of the seasons as perceived in the weather. In those days, well before biblical times, it was the Priests who understood astronomy. Stonehenge is probably the best-known example of an artificial horizon, over which the times of sunrise and sunset can be measured and events such as eclipses predicted.

The Sabbats of Samhain, Imbolc, Beltane, and Lammas (what Wicca calls "cross-Quarter days") were more important to herders and farmers. These Sabbats were marked and celebrated first. The astronomical moments we call Yule, Ostara, Litha, and Mabon were added to the calendar later on. That's why, and you've probably noticed this, the agricultural and astronomical calendars don't fit together exactly. Here's an example: Samhain is the Wiccan New Year, yet we say the Sun is reborn at Yule, and most of us don't notice the lengthening of the days until Imbolc! (On this book's side of the Wheel, Litha is mid-Summer, and according to some Wiccan Traditions, the God dies at Lammas, but we don't really see the days getting shorter until closer to Mabon.)

Another example is that in most Traditions, the Goddess gives birth to the Sun God at Yule. So when we say that She regains Her Maiden aspect at Imbolc, the implication is that She has given birth when She's a crone. Even though modern medical science has made it possible for real women to give birth quite late in life now, the idea of an old woman bearing a child still seems inconsistent to most experience.

The answer to these apparent problems is that the Wheel of the Year doesn't measure just the human cycle. Indeed, though it's based on real agricultural and astronomical cycles, the Wheel is a religious calendar, and so it's as metaphorical as it is literal. Otherwise, the Wiccans in the Southern Hemisphere would be—and they're not—wrong to celebrate mid-Summer in December and mid-Spring in October!

The human life cycle is but one of the many cycles that Wicca reveres. This also includes geological cycles, which are much longer than most of us can imagine. Naturally, we look for close correspondences between the Gods's stories and our own. After all, in Celtic mythology (a source of Wiccan lore), Gods and Goddesses are often spoken of as Kings and Queens. Anthropomorphizing the Gods is normal and obviously convenient, but it's possible to think of the Goddess and God too personally.

When we forget that They primarily represent the relationship of individuality to wholeness and the relationship of natural forces to the cycles of life, and when we also try to use Their stories as practical role models for male and female behavior, we can find ourselves unnecessarily confused. This doesn't mean, though, that there are no aspects of the Gods to which we can relate personally.

It's not wrong to imagine the Great Mother rocking us when we are needy, as a human mother might comfort her child. It's not wrong to think of the Horned One as our brother, encouraging us from His perspective to face death with a courage that comes from confidence in rebirth. But the Gods don't exist only for us or only in aspects convenient to our understanding. As Witches, we have both the capacity and the obligation to learn to know (and love and trust) Their other aspects as well. Remembering this and refraining from taking our metaphors too literally, we find the Wheel rolling more smoothly around the year for us.

This book looks at several aspects of the Summer holidays. Acknowledging that our mundane lives are lived in linear time, it examines each Sabbat in turn. This volume opens with a look at the lore surrounding each celebration, and continues with ritual celebrations and activities for solitaries, families, and covens. Finally, it ends with a discussion of the Wiccan symbols for each Sabbat. Another thing this book does is acknowledge that Wicca shares an Anglo-Celtic heritage with two other Neo-Pagan religions: Asatru and Druidry.

I won't go deeply into Norse mythology, but I'll note that as the Vikings made themselves at home in England, their religion adapted right along with them. Odin came to be known as Wotan, and Wayland the Smith became better known. Also, the Anglo-Saxon Runes, to which we'll refer, expanded the original Elder Futhark to accommodate sounds that Old English used and Old Norse didn't.

Though its modern forms are different than its ancient ones, Druidry is once again widely practiced and still embraces diversity as much as it did in the old days. There are several forms of Druidism, and it's ADF's Druidry that informs this book. (ADF stands for Ar nDraiocht Fein, pronounced *arn dray-okt fain*, which means "our own Druidry." It was founded by Isaac Bonewits, and it is the largest Neo-Pagan Druid organization in the world.)

Kirk Thomas, the liturgist for the Sonoran Sunrise Grove of ADF Druids says that "in ADF, we have many Norse, Roman, Hellenic, and Slavic members," and points out that they've all redeveloped Druidism differently. "I can only speak to Celtic ADF," he says. This is fine, because it's Celtic heritage that Wicca shares with Druidry.

It's important to understand that both Asatru and Druidry differ from Wicca in some significant ways, including the way in which ritual is conducted. For example, while the Asatru and Druids both tend to gather in circles, they don't work in "capital-*C*" Circles like Wiccans do. They also honor the Directions, but in different ways. The Asatru work almost exclusively with the Norse pantheons—primarily with the Aesir. (The Aesir are sky gods; the Vanir are earth gods. Worshipers of the Norse Vanir may distinguish themselves as Vanatru, but many accept the term Asatru as inclusive.) And rather than calling themselves Pagan or Neo-Pagan, most Asatru and Vanatru refer to themselves as Heathen.

Druids, of course, call themselves Druids. But liturgist Kirk Thomas explains something most people don't realize: "We are polytheistic, not duotheistic or pantheistic," he says. "We do not believe in a God and Goddess who have different aspects. Rather, each God and Goddess—and there are many—is a distinct and living personality, separate from the others." Some Wiccans also share this understanding of deity, but the introduction to the *Charge of the Goddess* shows us that Wicca's thealogy centers on the Mother Goddess and Her Consort, and considers Them each to have many aspects, which Wiccans know by various names. (The introduction to the first part of the *Charge* says, "Listen to the words of the Great Mother, who of old was known as…," followed by a long list of Goddess names—all of them belonging to Her.)

Throughout this book, you'll see not only how the Sabbats relate to each other, but also how the "big three" Neo-Pagan religions are related and how they influence each other. On virtually every page you'll be reminded that life is a cycle, to use a very human metaphor, and that each Sabbat is always balanced and supported by the others. Every Wheel, if it's to roll, needs all of its spokes and the whole of its rim!

> Winter's bright sword protects you,
> Summer's bright crown endows,
> and the turning Wheel perfects you,
> as by the spokes you make your vows.

Beltane

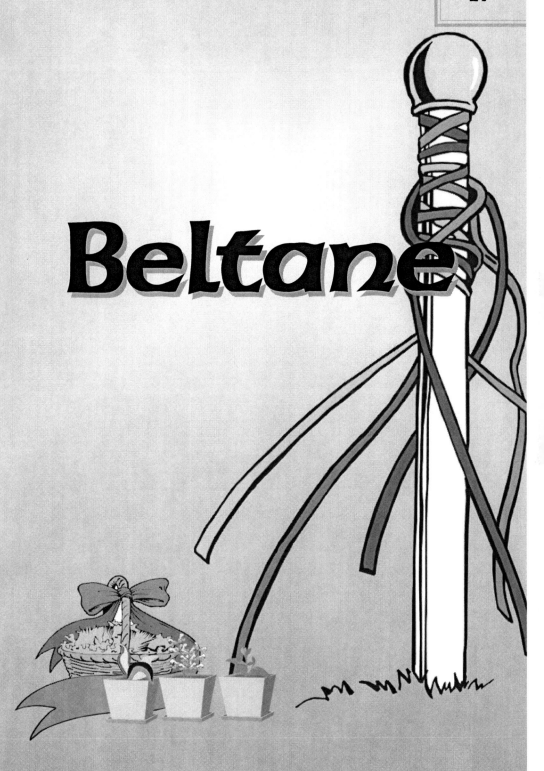

In the "old days," when our ancestors—Celts, mostly (the "Anglish" influence in our Anglo-Celtic heritage wasn't felt until 400 years later)—spread out across Western Europe and were still caring for their herds on the hills, the year was divided into two halves: Winter and Summer. Summer began around the time Wiccans identify as Beltane. By then, the weather in most places was warming up nicely, even in those years when Winter had been extremely hard.

The domestic livestock—cattle, goats, sheep, pigs—could be returned to their Summer pastures at about Beltane. Taking them out of the farmed pastures and up into the hills gave the fields a rest so that new crops could be nurtured and later harvested for Winter fodder. It also gave the beasts' caretakers time to tend the crops while the animals enjoyed themselves in natural feeding grounds.

Farming wasn't the only Summer occupation, though. Nor did fishing or hunting occupy all of everyone's time. With days getting longer and warmer, young people's fancies were turning—just like the Wheel of the Year. And we all know what they were turning to, don't we? Even if it's not one of your personal traditions to play Jethro Tull's "Songs from the Wood" at Beltane, you have some idea what's making the shrubbery shake (wink, wink, nudge, nudge).

Was the Maypole always a symbol of the union of the Goddess and God as it is for today's Wiccans? The answer is no. This is because original Goddess or Goddess-and-God worship had been pretty well wiped out even before the Inquisition, and doing folk magic for fertility wasn't attached to Pagan religion during the Middle Ages or the Renaissance. It was folk custom then and understood as such right up to the 20th century, according to Ronald Hutton in *The Triumph of the Moon*.

Beltane is a fertility festival. Mircea Eliade, the well-known religious scholar and philosopher, suggests in *Patterns in Comparative Religion* that Maypoles represent newly resprouted vegetation and that celebrations around them reflected people's joy in the plant world's strong return. There are lots of ways to interpret the meaning of the word *fertility*. Actually, *creativity*, being a broader term, might be a better word to use. We do like to honor our past, though, so most of us say "fertility" even if we haven't planted any crops and even if we don't hope to find ourselves in the family way. The symbolism of the Maypole is, if inoffensive, pretty obvious after all. (And come on, Professor Eliade, don't try to tell us that *nobody* in the old days noticed the Maypole's resemblance to other rising things than plant sprouts!)

On the other hand, there's obvious and then there's *obvious*. The Maypole at least slightly resembles the "world tree" that Druidic and Germanic tribes and modern religions see as linking our human realms with the Otherworld(s). The Norse called this tree Yggdrasil; the Anglo-Saxons called it Irminsul. There isn't any evidence that the Maypole was seen as a world tree in our cultural past, but that doesn't mean we can't give it that symbolism today. Just as our religion and its celebration of the seasons draws upon ancient and recent customs, it isn't limited to other times' understandings and faiths. Any and all of these interpretations of the Maypole—and all of them, I should think, more than any one interpretation in particular—are appropriate to Wicca.

We do love to think of medieval villagers dancing Maypoles. But when they did, they danced them very differently than we do today. There's evidence that huge trees were dragged into village squares and decorated with ribbons and garlands, and evidence that people danced and frolicked at the base of these trees once they were set up. Apparently, the occasional tent was seen at the base of a Maypole…and we don't think people were greenhousing seedlings in there either! Braiding the ribbons around the pole, though, is a modern custom dating back only about 100 years ago. Ronald Hutton in *The Stations of the Sun* says that although festivities took place at their bases, "[no Maypole dance] before the nineteenth century seems to have involved holding ribbons."

Nor is dancing the Maypole an unbroken tradition. It was intermittent for a long time, and not all that widely known either. In the 1600s, when the English government was torn between the monarchy and republicanism, Maypoles were frequently outlawed. Oliver Cromwell, a Puritan, hated the whole idea of the Maypole, considering it to be a Pagan abomination. While he was in power (between the reigns of King Charles I and Charles II) he outlawed Maypoles, but people managed to hide them right under his nose. Actually, they were hidden under the eaves of houses, where Cromwell's soldiers often failed to find them. Some poles left undiscovered were brought out again when the laws banning them were lifted. Indeed, in 1661, after the monarchy had been reinstated, King Charles II's brother, the Lord High Admiral, sent sailors to put up a Maypole, replacing one that had been removed in 1644 by the Republic under Cromwell's rule. The new one was 134 feet tall! Charles II rode past it on the way to his coronation, and it was, as Hutton tells us in *The Rise and Fall of Merry England*, "a focal point for the celebrations of the people of London and Westminster that summer and for fifty years after." (In case you wonder, if they *had* been dancing a ribbon braid around that pole, each ribbon would've had to have been about 50 yards long.)

Still, although it wasn't celebrated religiously then, fertility was honored and held holy—without it there'd be no new crops, no next generation of livestock, and no next generation of people. The economy, until the Industrial Revolution, depended on farming, animal husbandry, and cottage industries, as well as on inheritance and well-made marriages. So, bawdy as it may have been, fertility wasn't frivolous at all. It was, and still is in many places, a matter of life and death.

We feel today the same way about other sorts of fertility—creativity: It's holy. There may be nothing new under the Sun, but there's still plenty that's new to each of us and to our species, and it's our creativity that expands our perspectives and lets us understand things in ways that make them seem new. This is what Beltane is about. The wedding of the Goddess and the God (or perhaps faith and knowledge) celebrates not only the fertility of the earth and of our bodies, but the fertility of our minds as well.

Another element of Beltane is handfasting. Though some Traditions of Wicca place the wedding of the Goddess and God at Litha, many place it at Beltane. This Sabbat is a popular one for Wiccan weddings. A handfasting can't be considered a Beltane ritual, but many a fastening of the hands has taken place as part of a Beltane rite. Let's take a brief look at the basics and learn something about the ways in which the elements of handfasting relate to this Sabbat.

The following examples are taken from Adventure's *Book of Shadows*, but Wiccans of other Traditions will recognize many of the lines because they are common to Wicca as a whole. (The *Book of Shadows* belonging to Adventure was composed by me and my husband, the founding Elders of this particular Tradition. For more information about Adventure go to *www.adventurewicca.com*.) Non-Wiccan readers can get a fair gist of the ceremony, understanding that some details will differ among Traditions, eclectic clergy who perform these rituals, and the individual Wiccans who make personal contributions to their own rites.

A handfasting Circle is often physically defined with fresh flowers, dried rose petals, potpourri, birdseed, or ribbons. (Fewer and fewer weddings in any faith use rice now. It has long symbolized fertility, but it can be injurious to birds if they ingest it, and so it is falling out of favor. Birdseed makes a fine substitute.) Being able to see the Circle reminds us of much—from the circle of family and friends, generations, and experience that surrounds the bride and groom, to the circle our planet makes around the Sun, to the circular form Wicca's liturgical calendar takes to represent the Spiral Dance of Life.

The Goddess and God are invoked in Their maiden and youth aspects. Exuberance, romance, innocence, and potential are all important elements—of new relationships, of shared goals, and of Beltane itself. Yet a handfasting can last for more than a year and a day. It can be a lifelong commitment to a partner, and such a commitment might be said to circumscribe one's potential. Ah, but any choice at all precludes certain other choices: Before you finish reading this sentence, it has the potential—for you, at least—to conclude in an infinite number of ways. But now that you've begun reading *this* sentence, you know that the one preceding it can only end in one way. Its meaning, however, can continue to deepen and unfold for everyone who reads it, and its relationship to the truth of your experience still has infinite potential.

Doors close, doors open—and they don't always open on the same plane. When the door to a handfasting Circle closes behind the Happy Couple, so does a new door open to the commitment they're making to each other. A handfasting does, Canyondancer and I trust when we officiate at one, end the potential for wedded relationships to other people for the bride and groom, yet it opens a door to the infinite potential of the relationship the couple can have with each other. In much the same way, every Spring, some seeds sprout while some do not, and every Beltane sees a blossoming of some flowers, but not others. And yet those that *do* bloom have infinite potential to make the world joyful, to nurture our souls as well as those of the creatures of Nature, and to reseed the earth in their turn.

We've never yet performed a handfasting that didn't include some non-Pagans among the guests, so our ritual includes an explanation for them: We let people know that they'll see ritual space marked out and sanctified. We explain that they mustn't violate the boundary we draw around the space. So they'll be prepared, we tell them that the couple will leave the Circle by jumping a broom, we let them know how they'll know when it's time for them to leave the Circle, and we make them aware of what the respectful way of leaving is. We tell them that they'll hear invocations of the Goddess and God and the "Elements and energies we call holy," that the couple will receive blessings from the Quarters and from the Gods, and that the couple's wrists will be fastened by a consecrated Cord. Finally, we let them know that they're free to take photos—as long as they provide reprints for the bride and groom.

But it's the consecrated Cord I want to talk about in relationship to Beltane. In our Tradition, as in many others, we use a long, red cord because we consider red to be the color of life and love, and we hope that the couple's relationship will be lively and full of love—not just for each other, but for life itself. This Cord isn't as long as a Maypole ribbon or it'd take forever to wind around their wrists. Still, it's similar to a Maypole ribbon in some respects. Some of the instructions for dancing a Maypole apply not only to binding a couple with a handfasting Cord, but to living together in love as well.

For instance: When you dance the Maypole, you need to keep your ribbon tight enough so that it doesn't leave loops or lumps in the braid, yet not so tight that you pull the pole out of plumb. Likewise, when you fasten a couple's hands with their Cord, you want to make the binding tight enough to keep their flesh touching, but not so tight that you cut off their circulation. Also, in their relationship, the couple needs to be together enough to know each other well, yet separate enough to know themselves as individuals.

When you dance the Maypole, you need to be aware of the way other dancers are moving so people's distribution is roughly equal around the pole and so you don't get a crowd on one side or the other. But you need to pay the *most* attention to the way you are moving so that you're doing your part to maintain the pattern. (Just for the record, the proper movement is over, under, over, under—period. Not over or under one particular person each time, although this may vary according to the number of dancers. Over, under, over, under. It may sound boring, but it's entrancing, just as a relationship should be: supported by routines that free your mind for more esoteric enjoyments.)

As a couple's handfasting clergy, you have to be satisfied the bride and groom are responsibly and realistically committed, but you can't hold out for a guarantee that their love will blossom, any more than we can be sure that every blossom that opens at Beltane will be perfect and long-lasting. Each partner must hold a genuine interest in the other's growth and be truly supportive. Neither can or should control or inhibit the other's progress, and neither must neglect his or her own growth and progress either. Dancing the Maypole, you find that only a careful balance between attention to the other dancers and attention to your own footwork and ribbon-handling will result in the perfect braid you're looking for.

Is a perfectly braided Maypole possible? Absolutely, and I say so from experience. A perfect braid is an impressive and palpably energizing feat, even for the people left panting after the dance. Is a perfect handfasting possible? Yes, if you're flexible in your definition of "perfect" when it comes to the ritual itself; absolutely, if you're referring to the relationship that grows from the rite. Again, I speak from experience. (Canyondancer and I were conventionally married, sort of, the first time. I say "sort of" because the organist at our wedding accused us of choosing "Pagan" music, that being the traditional processional from *Lohengrin* and the traditional recessional from *A Midsummer Night's Dream*. We were finally handfasted on our 20th anniversary, and the whole 30 years have been filled with shared joys, sorrows, attainments, and griefs—in short, yes, perfect.)

For these and other reasons, I think that Beltane is a great time for a handfasting, and that, in a way, every Maypole dance handfasts us to life, the universe, and everything. I think that this is a great way to celebrate and recelebrate the seasons of life.

ORE

The name *Beltane*, which comes from marvelous-sounding Gaelic words, can probably be traced back to "the proto-Celtic god variously known as Bel, Beli, Balar, Balor, or the latinized Belenus," according to Janet and Stewart Farrar in *A Witches Bible Compleat*. In turn, these names derive from the Middle Eastern title *Baal*, which means "lord."

The god Bel was "the bright one." According to author Ronald Hutton in *The Stations of the Sun*, the common Celtic prefix *bel* "did indeed apparently mean 'bright' or 'fortunate.'" A god of fire and light, Bel was not—at least among the Celts, at any rate—a Sun god, for the Celts saw the Sun as feminine. Instead, Celtic gods such as Bel and Lugh had solar attributes. One of these solar attributes is the capacity to fertilize, to stimulate growth. The great bonfires at the beginning of Summer (Belfires, as many Wiccans still call them) represent the creative heat, the light and the warmth that bespeaks fertility of all kinds, from the fires we feel in our loins to forge-fires and the fires of poetic inspiration.

We must remember that the Goddess has Her fire aspects, too, particularly in the form of Brigid, a triple Fire Goddess. She is a healer, a smith, and a poet. Therefore, She is no stranger to fever-fires (including passion's "fevers"), forge-fires, and the fires of inspiration. Bel (or Lugh, or Llew, or Oghma) makes a fine Consort for Her, and Beltane is when, in many Wiccan Traditions, They celebrate Their union. Their marriage is sacred (we still use the Greek term *hieros gamos*) because fertility is sacred. Without it, we would be literally extinct. But it's not just the baby-making fertility that the Gods's marriage sanctifies.

Quoting Myles Dillon and Nora Chadwick, authors of *The Celtic Realms*, in their concise discussion of Irish history and political organization, the Farrars note in *A Witches Bible Compleat* that the sacred marriage of the Goddess and God was "a symbolic marriage with Sovereignty, a fertility rite for which the technical term was *banais rigi*, 'royal wedding.'" From this, we might consider that our celebrations of

Beltane replenish our personal power, maintaining our authority over our own lives.

Of course, in some senses, replenishment of personal power and maintenance of personal authority is part of every Sabbat celebration. Our choice to celebrate the seasons is itself an authoritative act. Certainly there are many people in the world who choose to be oblivious to their natural environments, and even their social environments. There are also people who choose to believe that our earthly life is insignificant or illusory. Neo-Pagans' choice to call the seasonal cycle holy and to participate as actively as we do in turning the Wheel of the Year is an assertion of personal authority and a recognition that our individual power is enhanced by the cooperation between each other and between the natural forces we hold sacred.

Preceding Beltane is Ostara, when the balance of the Year tips toward the light, toward activity (for which we've prepared during the reflective months of Winter). Although we—none of us—cause the movement of the universe, we—all of us—take a hand in guiding that movement so that, at Ostara, we can steer the changing balance, redefining our individuality as we re/emerge into the wider world of Summer. At Beltane, we "marry" our energy to the energy of other people and together become more powerful, like the Sun.

Litha, mid-Summer, follows Beltane. Then, corresponding to the Sun's achievement of zenith, our full-fledged individualities contribute to a full-strength community. Yes, we know that the Year's seasons don't correspond exactly to human experience: If our lives directly reflected the Year, none of us would live to be more than a year old! And although we do live our lives in identifiable cycles, the stages of our lives overlap more often than there is snow in May or balmy days in January. Furthermore, it takes some of us until the Autumn or Winter of our chronological lives to see the maturity that Summer symbolizes, while others of us reach that maturity before our chronological Spring has sprung. Nonetheless, the cycle of the Year shows us our individual potential, and offers us symbolically propitious opportunities to participate.

If dancing the Maypole is a community celebration, symbolizing the cooperative union of projection and reception, ensuring a group's successful cooperation, then jumping the Bel-fire is the corresponding individual act. Male and female alike jump the flames—for finding mates, ensuring projects' success, ensuring pregnancy and safe delivery, securing households from want, and to other creative ends. It can be difficult to get beasts—farm or domestic—to leap over dancing flames, so animals that cannot be carried over by a leaper were (and still are) either made to walk through the ashes of the Bel-fire or led between two fires.

The Fire gods and goddesses are naturally associated with Beltane—Bel (Lugh in His best-known Celtic form) and Brigid. Kirk Thomas, liturgist for the Sonoran Sunrise Grove of ADF Druids, tells us that at Beltane we can honor the marriage of the Gods with "any pair of lovers." He suggests a few pairs: "Diarmaid and Grainne, Pwyll and Rhiannon, Lleu Llaw Gyffes and Blodeuwedd," and says that which pair you prefer "depends on your pantheon."

Gamlinginn, a respected and experienced gothi (Asatru Priest) in New Mexico, in an unpublished article titled "Concerning the Modern Asatru Calendar," says, "One perceived 'gap' that the early Asatru revivalists felt necessary to fill had to do with the establishment of annual festivals to be celebrated on a regular frequency. Borrowing directly from Wicca, they decided that there should be eight of these.... One—May Eve—is entirely borrowed from Wicca." This is alright with Wiccans and Asatru alike: Nature's holidays can't be exclusively claimed by any of us, and no faith or culture can survive without making fertility sacred.

There is another Beltane tradition I find particularly charming, though hard to follow here in the desert where I live, and that's washing your face in May-morning dew. My aunt, whose parents' Scottish brogue was lilting but unintelligible to me and my parents, remembers hearing tell of it. And where I live, on those rare occasions when we've seen snow fall on Beltane morning at the higher elevations where my coven and our friends sometimes camped for a few days' celebration, we've happily taken the opportunity to bless ourselves with that chilly "dew." From a meadow's morning moisture, we can derive some benefits of the Otherworld: not immortality, but maybe lives longer by a day or two, a healthy glow, or perhaps a glimmer of the second sight.

The fairy associations with Beltane are many. My personal favorites are the legends of places in the British Isles where, if you spend the night, you'll wake up the next day insane or inspired. That is because those places are sacred to the local fairy tribe, and your fate depends on whether they look ill or kindly on your intrusion. Some say if you stumble onto or are invited to a fairy feast, you must not eat or drink anything. If you do, you'll be unable to leave—or when you do leave, you'll find that what seemed to be but a night of pleasure in fairy halls was actually scores of years in the mortal world.

But there are other tales of humans sojourning in fairy lands to great benefit. They come away with love or riches, or to find an injustice righted. Their crops or livestock may be forever blessed, or the catch from the sea always sufficient. It all seems to hang on two points: the human's purity of heart and his or her respect for the fairies, and that person's courage and manners.

In many Traditions, we conduct ourselves in Circle much as we would in a fairy palace. When our Circles are cast, they're declared to be "between the Worlds." We call our Priestesses and Priests Lady and Lord as we would address an Otherworld hostess or host, and we often call each other by fairy-like Craft names. When we enter our Circles to be initiated, we're challenged at the door and asked whether there is any fear in our hearts as we enter. Better it would be to rush upon the guardian's blade and perish, many of us are told, than to enter the Circle with fear in our hearts. Whether these liturgical customs were established with an intention to evoke the Otherworld or not isn't as important as the fact that they *can* and *do*. At Beltane, this is particularly the case (and with Litha too: Shakespeare's *A Midsummer Night's Dream* reflects the next Sabbat's connection with Fairy Land).

We know that Beltane is joined to Samhain by its position on the Wheel. Though Beltane marks for many Traditions the wedding of the Goddess and God, we can also see Beltane and Samhain as symbolizing the Goddess and God Themselves. In the Winter stories, it's the Goddess who descends to the Underworld, where She learns (is reminded) that the dead are not horrible creatures, but only lives resting in Her womb, awaiting their rebirth. As Summer begins, we can see that the God has come from the Underworld into Her realm of light and delight. The solar aspect of the God was reborn at Yule. His plant and animal aspects have enjoyed rebirth at Imbolc and Ostara, and yet it's not until Beltane that He's fully restored to His lusty, fertile, jovial self, the Green Man, the Horned One that we most often name and visualize.

The Ascent of the God

The God is our Fire, the Vine and the Beast;
the Goddess's son, and Her lover at feast.
He lives and He dies as circles the Year,
in both death and rebirth His fate always clear.
When harvest comes due, then He lays down His life,
grieving the Goddess as mother and wife.
Down through the grave His path guides His feet,
and in death comes to life a womb that's earth-sweet.
She follows Him there, He explains to Her fears;
He lightens Her heartache, He tempers Her tears.
She is reminded that sorrow's not all,
for grief's to endow Her glad-ringing hall.
She gives up life not, He dies only awhile:

In light He returns through Earth's
blessed aisle;

In green'ry resprouts, in flesh reappears,
and in May, with embraces and urges,
endears.

Deep separation deep marriage becomes,
Their rhythms like blooming; Their
heartbeats like drums.

He booms through Her realm as She wept
ent'ring His,

and They open the Gates to the forces of
bliss.

Long days from long nights grace this
bright period

when the Worlds celebrate the ascent of
the God.

Rituals

The best-known and most popular Beltane ritual is, of course, the dancing of the Maypole. I will share some lessons learned from experience (see "Maypole Tips"), but I want to emphasize that the deep physical delight of Beltane coupling isn't the only suitable celebration, nor is reproductive fertility the only sort of creativity we can and should encourage at this Sabbat.

It seems to me that Beltane is an especially appropriate time to introduce children to the rites of the Craft. Perhaps it's because children can see and pass through the doors to the Otherworld more easily than most adults can, or maybe it's because many depictions of fairies seem so childlike. Including children in our Beltane festivities reminds us that romantic love isn't the only joy, and certainly not the only physical exultation, worth recognizing as sacred.

Children ranging in age from 3 to 13 dance a Maypole dedicated especially to them.

Maypole Tips

1. For a 10–12-foot tall pole, use 18-foot long ribbons. This leaves enough extra ribbon after you've tied off the braid for everyone to cut off a piece to take home. Buy a variety of bright and pastels, two of each color, and a few patterned ribbons.

2. Delegate ribbon procurement to one person so you can be sure your ribbons will all be the same width and made of the same material.

3. You will need an even number of people divided equally into two groups, with each group dancing in the opposite direction of the other.

4. Lively music is a must. Pipe music, live or recorded, is fabulous. A strong beat helps.

5. The proper movement is over, under, over, under—period. Not over or under one particular person each time, although this can vary according to the number of dancers.

6. No one should change directions mid-dance.

7. Dancers need to keep their ribbons taut so that there won't be any lumps in the braid. However, no one should pull so hard as to tilt the pole.

8. If young children will be dancing, *set up a separate pole just for them*. Trust me on this one. If need be, a grown-up can join them to keep the number of dancers even.

9. Practicing ahead of time is a great idea. (Yarn works well for this purpose.)

Morning Ritual for Two-Year-Olds (and Inner Children)

From Hearth's Gate Coven Adventure Priestess Chandra Nelson, we have the following morning ritual for two-year-olds and the inner child in all of us. Teach it to your children at Beltane, and encourage them to use it throughout the year. Notice that it's a good morning stretch for grown-ups, too, and it is also a reverent way to greet each day with Beltane-like innocence and fullness of heart.

With arms overhead in a Sun-shape, say: "Blessed be this day, as I learn and play."

Spread arms open to each side. Putting your hands to your heart, continue: "Fill my day with love…."

Touch hands to the floor and then raise them overhead, and finish: "…from down below and up above."

This ritual self-blessing acknowledges all the Directions and serves as a quick grounding, opening you to the wonders of the universe and the day. The stretch feels good and can remind us, as Beltane itself does, that in order to have good health, we need to stretch our hearts, minds, and attitudes as well as our bodies. Blessed be May Day and every day!

May Baskets for the Lady and Lord

As virtually everyone is, I was aware of May Day traditions long before I was Wiccan. People older than I remember dancing Maypoles in their school yards, and I remember making May baskets with friends. Making them is so easy that you will not need to look to the section with activities for Beltane for directions. Simply get a basket, line it with paper shreds, and then fill it with one or two plants in small pots or with a riot of silk blossoms. Decorate the rim or the handle with ribbons, and there you have it! (A "mini-basket" can be made by rolling a gold or silver foil doily into the shape of a cone and then filling it with flowers.)

What I remember doing with May baskets is setting them on my neighbors' doorsteps or milk boxes, ringing the doorbell, and then racing away around the corner of the recipient's house to watch their expression of confusion turn into one of pleased surprise. In this ritual, you'll "ring the Gods's doorbell," so to speak, but you won't have to hide around the corner when They answer.

This ritual is easy for both solitaries and covens to do. It is even suitable, with minor modifications, for non-Pagans who just want to express their appreciation of Spring and Summer. (Remember, for Wiccans, Beltane marks the end of Spring and the beginning of Summer.) If you have a wand or a staff, you can use it to call the Quarters and invoke the Gods in your Beltane Circle, although you should still use your athame to cast it.

Before you begin, bring your May basket into the Circle and set it on or beside your altar at South. If there are several baskets, surround the altar with them. Whatever you use for Ale should be sparkling, and the Cakes should be extra-decorative—colorful sprinkles on white frosting would be appropriate, for instance. If you have a cauldron, place it on the outer edge of the Circle between East and South, and put a candle in it that is tall enough to be seen over its lip. If you do not have a cauldron, set up a small altar at that point instead.

If you are performing this ritual solitary, after you have cast your Circle (see Appendix A of *Celebrating the Seasons of Life: Samhain to Ostara* for directions if you haven't got a "usual way" of your own), carry the May basket around the Circle with you as you call the Quarters. If a coven is performing this ritual, then East should take the basket with great dignity from the altar area to his or her Quarter, and then ceremonially deliver it to South. As each Quarter-caller carries the basket to the next Quarter, he or she should continue walking deosil around the Circle until they return to the Quarter they called. Everyone's movement around the Circle should evoke a wedding party's procession down the aisle, for Beltane is, in many Traditions, the wedding day of the Gods. If you have two or three baskets, it might be fun to take each basket around in turn, especially if they were made by small children who would be disappointed if their basket wasn't included in the rite. If there are more than three baskets, though, for the sake of time, choose one to be taken around the circle, while the rest remain on the altar.

Once the Quarters are called and the basket(s) is returned to the altar area, a wand can be used to outline two arched doors in the center of the Circle. The Goddess will be invited to enter through a door facing Southeast, and the God will be invited to enter through a door facing Northwest. Once these doors have been cut with something of a flourish (imagine that magic is sparkling from the tip of the wand), invoke the Goddess and God like this:

> *Queen of the Summerland, Consort of Horn,*
> *be with us now where joy is born!*
> *We celebrate Your wedding day*
> *and all the glories of the fey.*
> *Join our Circle, bright and robust—*
> *Be welcome here in love and trust!*

If there are extra flowers on hand, sprinkle a few of the blossoms on the ground between the invocation doors. After a heartbeat's pause, take the God's candle from the altar and use it to light the candle in the cauldron or on the small altar at Southeast, and then return the God's candle to its original place.

Now to honor the Gods, present Them with all of the May baskets present. The Priestess should choose one basket, and, holding it up, give it her blessing. The Priestess's blessing for the May basket might be something like the following (if you are working solitary, deliver the following blessings yourself):

> *Basket of blossoms, heart of the May,*
> *breath and blush of the Queen of the Fey,*
> *with our good will, full spirited be:*
> *From our hearts to the Gods full blessings take thee!*

Next, the Priestess hands the basket to her Priest, who blesses it himself:

> *Basket of blossoms, from seeds begun,*
> *truth and track of the Horned One,*
> *with strong gladness brighter be:*
> *From our hearts to the Gods full blessings take thee!*

The chosen basket(s) is then passed around, giving everyone present a chance to bless the blooms. It's not necessary for everyone to have a rhyme prepared. It is enough for everyone to hold a hand over the basket, breathe upon it, or even blow it a kiss, and bless it silently or out loud. Blessings fit for a bride and groom are certainly appropriate, and so are blessings that reflect the gifts you're aware of having received from the Gods. It's even alright for people to tuck cards, preferably handmade ones that are small enough not to obscure the flowers, into the basket.

After the basket has been blessed, it is then presented to the Gods. The Priestess and Priest both carry the basket to the cauldron or small altar at Southeast and raise it overhead. (If you are working solitary, hold the basket in your left hand and your athame or wand in your right.) The words of presentation should be something like this:

> *Goddess-bride, my Lady fair,*
> *God-the-groom, green debonair,*
> *We hail You both, the sacred pair!*
> *We offer now our flowery care,*
> *life in love to always share:*
> *As You do will, so do we dare!*

The Priestess and Priest may speak these lines in unison, or everyone present might speak them in unison. Or, have the Priest speak the first two lines, everyone in the Circle speak the third, the Priestess recite the fourth and fifth lines, and everyone there join in on the last one. If you are performing the ritual alone, recite all the lines yourself. The basket should be placed in front of the cauldron or small altar as the last line is spoken.

During Cakes and Ale, special toasts may be raised to the Goddess and God. After that, the Circle should be closed as usual.

Beltane Vow

For many of us today, Summer is a time of vacation. School is out in most places, and most vacations are taken from work over the Summer months. So it was in the old days, too, to some extent. There was work to do in the Summer: fields had to be tended, and herds had to be watched and protected. When Summer's rains fell, there were dikes to build and irrigation ditches to dig. But longer days meant extra time to finish the season's work, or a little extra time to relax after the work was done. Pilgrimages were also generally undertaken in the warmer months, and while most pilgrimages were hard work (and meant to be), they were also a respite from the ordinary routine.

Vacations are meant to refresh us by relieving us of everyday responsibilities and recharging us with energy from new experiences. Pilgrimages also offer a break from routine—but don't let the association with Christianity and the Crusades put you off the idea of a pilgrimage. According to my old *Webster's New World Dictionary*, the word *pilgrimage* means "a [long] journey...especially to a shrine or holy place." Canyondancer's and my first trip to England to meet Wiccans we'd been corresponding with for years and to visit Robin Hood's grave was very much a pilgrimage as well as a revitalizing experience.

Revitalization is a theme at Beltane, both in the personal sense of renewal and refreshment gained, and in the community sense of reinvigorating and refertilizing life itself. This process occurs literally in the growth of fields and the fattening of herds, and symbolically as we braid the Maypole and represent our love of life in its brightly colored ribbons and the rhythms of the dance.

The rhythms of the Maypole dance are old, even if the custom of dancing it as we do now is not. Our 19th-century (cultural) ancestors may have been rather dour and even pessimistic, influenced as strongly as they were by dire religious perspectives, but for many more generations before us, the beginning of Summer was also symbolic of joy and optimism for the year and all who live in it. In calling upon the bliss of our ancestors, we're agreeing to find both sources of and places for joy in our lives, and in what we are heir to.

A fading cultural adage is that "ignorance is bliss," and most of us understand that this is not true. What we don't know *can* hurt us. But, more importantly, what we *do* know can enrich our lives with depths and textures we never imagined. Our ancestors (perhaps personally, certainly culturally) knew more about life and death, and of the close relationship between life and death, than many of us do today. Their nearness to death highlighted the days of their lives, just as the shade of an overhanging tree shows us both the colored pebbles of the streambed and the sparks of sunlight on the current's surface. Part of our species' legacy is to appreciate *all* the landscapes of our lives—outer and inner—with a vision made clearer by our awareness of the seasons' turning. Ignorance of the ribbons in our hand or of the spiraling May-dance paths we walk is no sort of bliss at all, but rather misery.

The May dance takes you over and under: Let's call this "over" the delightful face of the Earth, through the mundane world that your will can make both glad and bountiful, and "underground" to the Fairy Land, where the treasures of your own inner strength are warded. The May dance takes you 'round and 'round, just as the seasons roll. And just as your ribbon is not wrapped around the same length of pole twice, neither are you held back from growth except by the hesitations in your own steps. In what has been left to you by those whose lives are the foundation of yours, there is example enough of joy and bliss enough for you to follow.

Take Beltane's vow before you dance the Maypole (if you're lucky enough to find one in the center of your Circle). Otherwise, take it before you go to a fabric store to select a trio of ribbons that you can braid for yourself as a reminder of your passage through the seasons and the world, and also as a token of the delight that can always mark your path. There's room for you to fill in a word or two so you can dance to fulfill your own needs and dreams:

On the Wheel of the Year now does Summer begin:
the world is beribboned, a gay harlequin.
My heart I will open, delight I'll empower,
that in all of my steps, _____ shall flower.
I vow to go dancing, I now promise this:
To invoke and release my ancestors' bliss.
This task I do claim as I mark this Beltane,
and swear't by the magical and the mundane.

ctivities

Dancing the Maypole is the best-known Beltane activity, but not everyone has the opportunity to arrange it. Happily, there are other activities that everyone can enjoy that almost equally capture the spirit of the day. That spirit goes beyond the wink, wink, nudge, nudge interpersonal merrymaking that makes Beltane so popular, and includes creativity of all sorts, along with an openness to the Otherworld that can further inspire us.

While Samhain is popularly associated with the dark side of the Otherworld and with the serious responsibilities that come with what we might call the transdimensional power of Fairy Land, Beltane is more often associated with its lighthearted and wondrous aspects. We may swallow hard before we part the Veil at Samhain, but, at Beltane, we're through with just a hop and a skip.

A Veil Between the Worlds

One way to symbolize the Veil Between the Worlds and our passages through it is to make a veil! You'll need a tension rod with a small diameter. It should be long enough to span a hall or a doorway in your home, or to fit between patio pillars if you'll be using it outside. Garden arches also make a lovely support for a veil!

You'll also need a piece of netting, either nylon net or tulle, that is twice as long as the distance between the floor and the height at which you will be placing the tension rod. Make sure your netting is wide enough to cover the length of the rod. White, gold, or silver are the best colors to choose for your fabric (with these colors, you'll be able to use your veil at Samhain also, if you want to).

Fold the length of net or tulle over the tension rod with an equal amount of netting hanging on either side. Secure the fabric to the rod with matching thread, yarn, or embroidery floss. In a pinch, staples or safety pins will do. Next, lay the tension rod on the floor and spread the netting out on either side. With scissors, cut each panel of the veil into two vertical strips. From the bottom, cut your strips nearly to the top, but do not cut all the way to the rod. The strips do not need to be of equal width. Try to offset them a little on each side so that once you hang the rod, the strips will overlap each other. Neither the net nor the tulle should fray, but if you want to, you can trim all the long edges with narrow rickrack, sequined trim, or with anything else that's not too heavy. Again, gold, white, or silver are the best colors for any edging.

O'Gaea steps through a veil made of white tulle and silk garlands, which hangs from a tension rod in an interior doorway.

To decorate your veil for Beltane, use silk flowers or other adornments that trail or dangle. Silk wisteria, ivy, and bridal notions are good, for they're all graceful with gentle movement. Take a trip to your local craft store and look around. You can also find appropriate decorations in party stores. For instance, silk leis cut into shorter lengths work well. Save a few blossoms to sew or glue onto one side of the veil to look as if they had drifted down.

You can choose to decorate both sides for Beltane, leave one side plain, or decorate the second side for Samhain, when it would be appropriate to turn the veil and use it again. You can incorporate your veil into Beltane or Samhain rituals as you see fit. In the meantime, hang it in a doorway or across a hall on May Day to remind yourself that the realm of Faerie is always open to you and to give yourself permission to enter it and bring back a renewed sense of joy from your visit.

Maybe you don't have a hall or a doorway where you're comfortable hanging up a veil, or maybe you have the ideal place but your pets make the project impractical! Never mind. There are other things you can do to evoke the sense of a veil. One such activity is making fairy flags.

Fairy Flags

Once you are done making your fairy flags, you can display them like Yule cards on your walls, taped or strung along bookcase shelves, or even attached to the fridge with magnets. Tape them up on doors, behind the glass panels on cabinet doors, or anywhere else in your home where they can brighten your days and your thoughts.

Make them out of tissue paper in bright colors and patterns. Each flag should be about 8-inches wide and about 12–14-inches long. Make them longer if you'd like to shape the bottoms in curves, points, or crenellations. You can fold them like paper dolls and cut designs into them, or you can create designs on them with glue and glitter. Once any glue you've used is quite dry, hang up your flags!

Where else can you put them? You can hang them in your garden right from plants (use the very small clothespins found in craft stores—they're so small they won't hurt most plants and they come in bright colors to match or contrast with your flags), or hang them from strings taped to fences or garden poles. If you have decorative lights strung on your patio, fairy flags can be attached between the bulbs.

There is a Mexican influence in these flags, which is not surprising, because I live just about 60 miles from the Mexican border and have long taken great delight in the similar flags I see displayed here for a variety of festivals. But our fairy flags have a twist. In addition to decorating them with cutouts or glitter, we can also attach lengths of colored curling ribbon to each side of them. On these ribbons, we can write a few words of appreciation for the inspiration we have received from the Otherworld.

For Wiccans, these ribbons can symbolize the Maypole's ribbons, their colors standing for the same qualities, and each individual's choice of colors a declaration of their openness to their particular blessings. Flying the flags welcomes the Sidhe into our lives, and the colored ribbons we decorate them with pledge our attention to and appreciation of their blessings.

Fairy Dust

Some of us live in places and circumstances where any bright displays might be problematic. Though, generally speaking, non-Pagans do like May Day and find its celebration more quaintly endearing than threatening. We can still make fairy dust, though, and use it privately.

All you need is some talcum powder and some colored sugar, which you can find in your grocery store. You may also use a bit of glitter if you'd like. Mix the powder and the sugar together, add glitter if you want, and voilá! You have fairy dust. There are other "recipes" for it too: You can use finely ground cornmeal instead of talcum powder, or even whole-wheat flour.

If you use cornmeal or flour with the colored sugar, you don't have to worry about where the dust lands because it's organic and nontoxic. Yes, alright, the sugar might be a bit pokey if the fairy dust falls in your underwear or your socks, but the worst that'll happen is that your sweat will dissolve it, possibly leaving a small colored mark on you or your clothes. Call it a fairy touch and let it inspire you according to the symbolism of that particular color!

May-Morning "Dews"

The following is an article originally written for the Ostara/Beltane 2004 issue of the Tucson Area Wiccan-Pagan Network's quarterly newsletter, *Tapestry*, by Adventure Priestess Chandra Nelson, in which she talks about the old tradition of washing your face in May-morning dew. Thanks, Lady Chandra!

> *The fair maid who, the first of May*
> *Goes to the fields at break of day*
> *And washes in dew from the hawthorn tree*
> *Will ever after handsome be*
> —Mother Goose

Okay, if hawthorns aren't available, the outside temperature doesn't reach the dew point, and/or getting up at dawn is impractical, what's a maiden to do? Here are some alternatives to the famous May dew that will help keep your complexion beautiful.

If you don't have dew, try steam! Boil two cups of water. Add two or three drops of lavender essential oil, two or three sliced strawberries, and one teaspoon of red clover leaves (from capsul or tea bag from a health food store). Turn off the heat, drape a towel over your head, and hold your face over the steam six to eight inches away. This will help open pores and remove impurities. Lavender brings happiness, peace, and love (what is more beautiful than that?) and strawberries and red clover also bring love.

Here's a good facial cleanser: Grind one cup of oatmeal, one quarter cup at a time, in a coffee grinder. Put the oat flour in a sealable container. Next, grind two tablespoons dried lavender to a powder. Add to the oat flour. Add a tablespoon of betonite clay, if you wish. Mix well. To use, wet your face, take approximately a tablespoon of the powder in your hand and add warm water to make a paste, and massage the paste over your skin. Rinse well. Oats hold in moisture, lavender has antibacterial properties, and clay tones the skin. Oats bring prosperity, and bentonite brings love and clarity, while clay in general suggests creation.

And here's a lovely toner. This one is wonderfully easy to make; the only two ingredients are rose water (found at health food stores and some drugstores) and witch hazel (found at grocery and drugstores). For dry or mature skin, mix two parts rose water to one part witch hazel; for combination skin, a 1:1 ratio; and for oily skin, one part rose water to two parts witch hazel. Store in a bottle or jar and apply to your face with a cotton ball. Rose water helps to restore your natural moisture balance, while witch hazel is an astringent with antibacterial properties. Roses, of course, mean love and beauty, while witch hazel brings protection and power.

Wand of Discovery

The popular image of using a wand comes from movies such as Walt Disney's *Cinderella*, in which the Fairy Godmother makes things happen simply by waving one. Oh, golly, don't we wish! For most Wiccans, though, a wand is for inviting and guiding energy—a more gentle Tool than the athame, which most often commands. But the wand performs another function, appropriate for children as well as for adults, and that's *discovery*. A wand's work is to "draw attention to," and this is not always in terms of drawing attention or energy to *work* magic. Sometimes the idea is to draw attention to a magic that has *already* been worked.

When we point a wand at something, we might be guiding working energy toward that object or we might be directing awareness to that object, pointing it out as already magical. This last purpose is the exclusive function of a wand of discovery, making it an ideal craft for both children, who can always use validation of their natural talent of seeing things as magical, and adults, who often need reminding to see things as magical. Best of all, a wand of discovery is easy to make.

You will need a wooden dowel, the narrowest you can find. Sometimes you can get a 36-inch long piece where lumber is sold, but, more reliably, you can find it in a craft store. (You're looking for something less than a 1/4-inch wide in diameter.) If you can't find a wooden dowel, wire will do—and you can find wire in nearly any hardware store. But if you're using wire, it's imperative to make a handle for the wand so that you are protected from any sharp edges!

For each wand, you will need a length of dowel or stiff wire to match the distance between the tip of your middle finger and the pointy bone in your elbow. You will also need some craft glue, pony beads, glitter, bits of ribbon, and perhaps some leather scraps to make a handle. You may also use very small bells or small faux flowers. Use a bead or two to make a tip for the wand, and decorate the rest any way you like. Allow plenty of time for the glue to dry before you use your wand.

Explain carefully to small children that the wand is not to be used for things such as poking pets or batting siblings. If it's ever used that way, remove it from the offending wielder immediately—matter-of-factly rather than angrily—and allow him or her to try to use it properly the next day. This teaches not only respect for pets and siblings, but also respect for magical Tools.

For those who haven't the opportunity to go out and buy the materials for this project, try making a wand out of a piece of rolled paper, using glue, tape, string, or a rubber band to keep it from unrolling. You can color the paper with markers or crayons before you roll it, or you can glitter it afterwards. A paper wand won't be as durable as one made of wood or metal, though, so expect to make a new one every Beltane or whenever necessary.

Use this wand to discover the magic in the world around you. Touch the stems of blooming roses with it, and say, "Beauty is magical." Point toward fluffy clouds with it, say what objects their shapes remind you of, and then say, "Imagination is magical." Wave it through the air as if it's dancing, dance yourself while you wave it, and recognize that "motion is magical." Listen to music on the radio or stereo and use your wand of discovery like a conductor's baton. Learn that "music is magical." Touch the leaves of the vegetables in your garden and discover the magic in both growth and food. Touch the soil and discover the magic in plain ol' dirt! Touch the bubbles in the bathtub, for water and cleansing are magical. Touch the image in the mirror and discover the magic in yourself.

Don't stop there, and don't think you must have your wand with you to recognize the different magics you encounter every day, in every aspect of your life. At work or school, imagine yourself holding the wand, and think what you could touch with it there. Language itself, speaking and reading, is magical; it lets people communicate complex ideas, share information over time and distance, and connect cultures and generations. Wow! Computers are magical, too, aren't they? What about the cooperation it takes to complete a class or an office project? Or the patience it takes to deal with a difficult schoolmate or coworker? Things such as cooperation and patience are hard to touch with a physical wand, but you can touch them with the wand in your mind and recognize them as being magical.

Beltane Recipes

Where I live, it's usually warm enough by Beltane that we're looking for cool meals, or at least dishes that don't require much baking, as warming up the oven heats the whole house. Here are a few recipes for this season.

Peach Shortcake

For sweet treats, find little sponge-cake cups—not the molds, but the actual cup-shaped cakes—in your store. (They make an excellent base for more than strawberry shortcake, which I think is better suited to Lammas than Beltane). Next, make peach puree by chopping fresh or canned peach slices into small pieces and blending the heck out of them until they are the consistency of applesauce. (Use either a blender or a food processor for this.) Fill the cups with the peach puree, and top them with whipped cream, homemade or store-bought; honey; or with a little sugar. Quick and easy, these treats are satisfying whether the peach puree is chilled or at room temperature.

Peach Leather

Another treat to make with peach puree is fruit leather. This isn't at all difficult, but it does take a day or so if you want to avoid using your oven.

Spread your peach puree thinly on a cookie sheet lined with wax paper or plastic wrap, and cover the whole thing with cheesecloth or a towel, being careful not to let it sag into the puree. Set it aside to dry out. I think it's nicer when it is sun-dried, but you do want to keep bugs and plant-bits out of it, so to dry it in the sun, you do want to cover it. Hereabouts, leaving it out for a day is usually long enough; check yours in the morning to see if your climate's had long enough. If you do this in the oven (without the cloth and using wax paper instead of plastic wrap, of course), you'd put it on low heat and check it every hour or so until it gets leathery.

When it is dry, it should look dark and leathery. To enjoy your peach leather, simply tear off bits and munch on them. If it's too tart for you, put a touch of honey on it. You can also try rolling up a piece with honey or a bit of whipped cream inside.

Fairy Kebab Wands

No, this isn't about barbecue! It is about sugar, so indulge in moderation. You will need a bag of miniature marshmallows and a packet of small, wooden kebab skewers. If you can find marshmallows in pastel colors, so much the better. If you can't, not to worry: Dip them in marshmallow cream or honey, and roll them in colored sprinkles. Make sure you give them plenty of time to dry on wax paper on a flat surface.

To make the fairy kebab wands, all you have to do is push four or five marshmallows onto the end of a kebab stick, and there you have it! If you're making these ahead of time for a party, you can dress them up even more by painting the holding-end of the kebab sticks gold or silver, but make sure to leave the tip unpainted so the marshmallows don't touch it.

Frozen-Yogurt Floats

You already know how to make floats, I'm sure, so this isn't as much a recipe as it is a reminder of what a delightful beverage this is. They're refreshing all Summer—from Beltane right through Lammas, and until the end of August!

All you need is some fat-free vanilla frozen yogurt and your favorite soda. I suggest frozen yogurt for this treat because it is a fat-free alternative to ice cream. I used to make a face when anyone suggested substituting fat-free frozen yogurt for real ice cream. Then, after Canyondancer's heart attack, we got serious about reducing the fats in our diet, and rather than giving up my ice cream, I took a deep breath and tried the fat-free frozen yogurt. You won't be depriving yourself of any flavor, I promise!

People argue about whether to put the frozen yogurt in first and pour the soda over it, or whether to put 1–2 inches of soda in the bottom of a tall glass, add a hefty scoop of frozen yogurt, and then fill the glass with more soda. I think it works well both ways, so I guess you'll just have to try it more than once to decide which tastes best to you!

ymbols

"Sabbat symbols" can take one of at least two forms. A symbol can be a sort of shorthand notation for a concept associated with a particular Sabbat. For example, ♥ and ❀ are common symbols for love, a concept linked to Beltane. The same goes for ↗, which is associated with Cupid and, therefore, love. A symbol may also take the form of an object closely associated with a Sabbat. Let's take a look at a few objects associated with Beltane.

Butter Churn

Though it may be obscure, a butter churn is a symbol of Beltane, and a moment's thought will tell you why. The churn itself symbolizes the Goddess's womb, and the handle represents the God's phallus. While the churning of butter (or the plowing of fields) may be a rather crude mimicry of animal coupling, the fact that it effects a transformation of milk into butter is an excellent representation of and reminder that fertility, and every other form of "creativity," *is* transformation.

Fairy Royalty

Fairies are associated with both Beltane and Litha, but it's at Beltane that I think we have the best chance of seeing them. Beltane is across the Wheel from Samhain, and, for most of us, it's our second most sacred Sabbat; the Veil Between the Worlds is thinnest at these two times of the Year.

Let me make one thing clear: When I say that Samhain and Beltane are our two most sacred Sabbats, I don't mean that the other Sabbats are significantly less important or that we don't celebrate them as sincerely. It's only that Beltane, like Samhain, celebrates the beginning of an original season. Beltane, like Samhain, is not only a very down-to-earth commemoration, but also marks a time when our awareness of other dimensions is heightened. Thus, Beltane, like its Winter counterpart, celebrates the integration of spirit and matter, which is fundamental to Wiccan belief. This unity is part of every Sabbat, but the folklore and customs from which Wicca draws most heavily associate it a little more with Samhain and Beltane.

Fairies are among the best-known ambassadors of the Otherworld (Fairy Land is one of its names, as well as one of its realms), and so the fairy is among the symbols of Beltane. Inspired by the ceremony of the Goddess and God's sacred marriage, we often think of fairy royalty at Beltane in particular.

Oberon and Titania are the names Shakespeare gave to the King and Queen of the Fairies in the delightful comedy *A Midsummer Night's Dream* (which also illustrates that Beltane shares its fairy associations with Litha). It's often suggested that the Irish fairies, at least, used to be recognized as gods, but were crowded out of this world and into their underground palaces by a combination of defeat, trickery, and civilization's "progress." Maeve (also spelled Medb) was a warrior-queen of Connacht, but may have been fairy royalty as well, for no man could be Connacht's king without marrying her: She may be the embodiment of the land itself, and thus a goddess or fairy queen. From the Arthurian legends, we remember Morgan le Fay (Morgan the Fairy) who has as legitimate a claim to fairy monarchy as any.

Fairy Rings

What is a fairy ring? As the term is most commonly used, to mundane sight, it's an unexplained circle of mushrooms or a circle of taller grass; maybe a circle of wild flowers. No one planted them that way. There is no immediately obvious explanation for the growth of these plants in that form, but there they are! Perhaps it even appears to be a little track where a mouse or vole has run in dizzy circles for some reason we two-legs can't begin to fathom. The "capital-*O*" Other explanation is that these rings are where fairies have been dancing. With so many creatures of both worlds celebrating the warmer weather and fertile promises of Beltane, this is when we're most likely to come across fairy rings. Resembling flower crowns as they do, they've become a symbol of this Sabbat.

A fairy ring might also be a piece of jewelry worn by fairies—or the gods. At Midsummer, some say the fairies come out of the mounds and into our realms, but you can only see them looking through the ring of the Irish love and fertility goddess Aine.

Flower Crowns

Flower crowns are also symbolic of Beltane. They're wedding garlands, of course. And to think of it, it is popular to hold Pagan weddings at Beltane. Indeed, handfastings themselves can be symbolic of Beltane. Wiccan brides and grooms both traditionally wear flower crowns, as well as their best robes or even fancier garb.

What flowers are the crowns made of? Anything that is blooming at the time, providing its stem is flexible and not too fragile or gooey. White and yellow flowers are favored, but pink ones add a nice "blush" of color to any crown. These days, you can buy garlands made of silk flowers, allowing you to combine the blossoms of a variety of plants, whether or not they are native to your area. When wild or garden flowers aren't available, silk flowers work just fine.

Generally speaking, red flowers stand for passionate love, pink for more gentle affection, and white for chastity or fearlessness (both qualities associated with the Goddess's Maiden aspect). Yellow flowers traditionally represent less noble feelings, such as jealousy and scorn, but we Pagans can think of yellow blossoms as reflecting the Sun's golden rays. Ivy is a symbol of fidelity and stability in marriage, and by extension in any relationship. Buds of any flower bring the excitement of unrestricted potential to a bouquet, garland, or crown.

Daisy chains are probably the most common garlands and crowns. Daisies are ubiquitous, and the chains are easy to make. Divination by daisy is also a well-known practice: What schoolchild hasn't plucked the petals, one by one, wondering whether "s/he loves me" or "s/he loves me not"?

Foxglove has strong associations with fairies and with magic—and why not? It's a medicinal plant, too, and medicine has always been considered a kind of magic. Foxglove has many fairy names, including fairy bells, fairy gloves, and fairies' petticoat. Unfortunately, it's not an easy flower to weave into a garland.

Hawthorn is known as May bush, and it's considered to be magical, a Goddess-flower. Two or more hawthorns growing together form, in some lore, a gateway to the Otherworld. You have to be careful of this, and also of the thorns, of course, but the white flowers and sturdy stems make it a good base for flower crowns.

The Green Man

The Green Man is the foliate form of the God, and while this image is appropriate to Ostara and Litha as well as to Beltane, it's probably most strongly associated with Beltane. Other forms of the God also correspond with Beltane. The stag, along with His other aspects, is commemorated in the *Song of Amergin*, which begins, "I am the stag of seven tines...." Another way to think of the Green Man is as a "twin" of the Jack-o'-Lantern. Indeed, another name for the Green Man is Jack-in-the-Green.

A homemade Green Man mask honors the God's foliate aspect.

The Maypole

Of course, the Maypole is the first thing most of us visualize when we think of Beltane. It remains a relatively inoffensive symbol too, despite its rather obvious "hearty" connotations. The Maypole itself is phallic, although it represents the thrusting growth of saplings, vines, and other plants as much as it does the erect animal penis. The ribbons that decorate the pole represent the many varied forms life takes, and the many qualities that combine variously to make each life-form unique. Braided, the ribbons encase the pole, the same way a female's genitalia embraces that of the male, and just as the warm, bright air of the world receives vegetation as it comes forth from the earth.

Overall, the Maypole and the braid we dance around it symbolizes the balanced cooperation that is required for life, and any of us living it, to succeed and grow. It is a forthright demonstration of just how beautiful that cooperation can be, and how magical it can feel. Anyone who has ever seen ready ribbons rippling in the breeze on a sunny Beltane morning or run their eye down the hues of a well-braided pole can affirm this from experience.

Mirrors

Mirrors symbolize Beltane too. Why? Well, mirrors have always seemed like portals to other worlds—if no other examples come to mind, think about Lewis Carroll's *Through the Looking-Glass*. At Beltane, the weather is beginning to be lovely: Things are blossoming, sweet fragrances fill the air, the clouds are fluffy, animal families are cavorting, and the world is young and wonderful. A mirror in a field or meadow at Beltane would reflect something very similiar to what we imagine the Summerland to look like. If you were able to step through that mirror, you might find yourself in the Land of Youth! So in their portal aspect, mirrors are symbols of Beltane and the Otherworld Beltane reflects.

Litha

It is easy to think that Litha is exclusively about the Sun and the God in His solar aspect. After all, Litha—mid-Summer—is, in the Northern Hemisphere, the longest day of the year and the time when the Sun is as far north in the sky as it will ever get. However, just as the Sabbat of Litha is significant in relationship to the other Sabbats, the Element of Fire, which is central to Litha celebrations, is also significant in relationship to the other Elements. Water, which can be viewed as Fire's opposite, has its own significance to Litha.

The seasons we celebrate aren't disconnected. Instead, they are stages of becoming. Although we physically perceive them sequentially, we understand them religiously not as linear, but rather as cyclical. This is why the Wiccan calendar is a Wheel: We see the seasons as rolling. So even though Water is, on most tables of correspondences, associated with Autumn and the West, it's an important element in Litha rites as well.

Before we look at Water's significance to Litha, let's take a quick look at how the other Elements relate to Fire. The Elements are associated with the Solstices and Equinoxes. Litha is the Summer Solstice, and across from it on the Wheel is Yule—the Winter Solstice. Yule (Winter, North) is associated with Earth. Ostara and Mabon, the two Equinoxes, are associated with the Elements of Air and Water, respectively. This means that Litha's Fire is "opposed" by Earth—though "complemented" is a more useful way of putting it—and surrounded by Air and Water.

We can understand Earth and Fire balancing each other: Not only are most fires built upon earth itself or on a framework of material associated with it, but if you're on fire physically, you "stop, drop, and roll," which is to say, you counterbalance the fire with earth. If you've raised too much energy in Circle—if you're "burning" in that sense—you "ground" by reconnecting with the Element of Earth. Beyond that, whether we sprout from it, crawl on it, or walk upon it, the planet Earth is our anchor. It is what supports and orients us.

We understand Air as being essential to Fire—nothing burns in the absence of air. Symbolically, the beginnings, the ideas, and the thought processes Air (East) represents are necessary to inspire the passions that "burn" within us. So Fire's relationship to Earth and Air and Litha's relationship to the Sabbats that precede it are relatively easy to understand.

But Water? Water puts out Fire, but you might ask yourself how this can be part of the Litha celebration of the Sun's fiery strength. In the Farrars's *A Witches Bible Compleat*, it's suggested that fire is the God's aspect and water is the Goddess's aspect.

It's one of my pet peeves that most calendars call June 21 (or there-abouts, depending on the time of the Solstice, which varies from year to year) the "beginning of Summer." Traditionally, the Solstice marks the midpoint of its season. Hence, Shakespeare named his play *A Midsummer Night's Dream* rather than *The Beginning of Summer Night's Dream*! (On Wicca's calendar, Summer begins at Beltane.)

The name *Litha* comes from the Anglo-Saxons. According to *An Anglo-Saxon Dictionary* (Oxford University Press, 1898), the month of June was known as "Aerra Litha"—meaning "before Litha"—and what we call July was known as "Aefter Litha." Drawing on Anglo-Saxon as he did on many old Germanic languages, J.R.R. Tolkien made a single reference to mid-Summer as "Lithe" in the *The Fellowship of the Ring*, the first book of *The Lord of the Rings* trilogy.

We should note that the spelling of *Litha* wasn't the same then—the Anglo-Saxon alphabet was slightly different. In those days, between about 500 and 1200 C.E., it would've been pronounced *lee-tha*, with the *th* sounding like it does in *thou*. A minority of Wiccans today say *lee-tha* or *lih-tha*, pronouncing the *th* as in the word *think*. Most pronounce it *lee-ha*. And although we may speculate as to its meaning or even assign it a meaning in the context of our Traditions, there is no other listing in the dictionary for the meaning of the word Litha other than in relation to the names of the months.

There is no speculation required to know that the Summer Solstice is the moment of the Sun's zenith—when it is, from Earth's perspective, as far north as it will ever get, and to our eyes, as high in the sky. In the Northern Hemisphere, the day of the Summer Solstice is the longest day of the year, when we have the most hours of daylight. Other than we can play outside until 10 p.m. (later in some places), what does this mean?

For Wiccans, the Sun is a symbol of the God. Some of us may believe that the Sun itself is a god, but most of us understand the Sun to be a physical representation of an aspect of the God—the solar aspect! The rays of the Sun have long been seen as fertilizing: When clouds make the rays visible, slanting to Earth in golden beams, it looks like the Sun is reaching out to us, touching us with the warmth and light that living things need to propagate.

Generally, Wiccans perceive the God as active and the Goddess as receptive. Physically, the Sun radiates its own light and warmth, while the Moon reflects the Sun's light. This does not mean that She basks in His glory: In our cosmology, the material plane is only symbolic of the metaphysical. And, anyway, realities and polarities reverse in progression from physical to metaphysical planes. At the Summer Solstice, the Sun's radiation, literally and figuratively, is at its peak. His activity in the physical world is obvious and intense. This is especially true in southwestern states such as Arizona, where unless we temper the Sun's godly enthusiasm with sunscreen and shade, we are in danger of becoming the burnt offerings our Goddess doesn't ask for!

Yet even as the Oak King's strength is at its greatest, He is challenged by Holly, by the oncoming Winter. At Litha, it can be difficult to remember or imagine Yule's comparative chill and darkness. But, from the Summer Solstice on, there is no denying that the Year is rolling toward Winter. It may also seem as though the Summer and Winter Solstices are opposites, for these Sabbats are across from one another on the Wheel. But "opposite" implies opposition, and, in fact, Litha and Yule cooperate, for the Oak and Holly Kings that personify these holidays are brothers.

Summer's King, the Oak King, is the Goddess's Consort—Her lover and Her partner in fertility and abundance. Remember, it's in His Green Man aspect that He marries the Goddess at Beltane. As Beltane's Green Man, He is younger, His foliate face composed of the leaves and buds of many plants. By Litha-tide, as the Oak King, He's represented by one tree. In superficially the same way, we too often have many options in our youth, and by our maturity we have focused our lives on one theme.

By Lammas, to continue the foliate metaphor, His leaves have begun to turn. The Oak's leaves aren't dry and brittle yet, but their green is tinged with the colors of Autumn. Though there is just a hint of what is to come in His face, it is visible on His branches that His death—no, let's be accurate rather than poetic and say "transformation"—is inevitable. So, too, are the days getting just a little shorter now; across the Wheel from Lammas, at Imbolc, is when we begin to notice the days getting longer. Across the Wheel from Litha, Winter is in full strength, just as Summer's full power is marvelously evident in the Oak King's Solstice heat.

Summer's King is also the Goddess's son, born to Her at Yule. The Oak King's relationship to Holly—Litha's relationship to Yule—is among the trickiest correlations in Wiccan cosmology. We tend to want to understand it all in human terms—this is why we speak of Oak and Holly Kings, and why we personify the Gods at all.

Rick Johnson, a Gardnerian British Traditional Priest in Tucson, develops the metaphor this way:

> "...at Litha, the Sun God, battling Himself, is wounded, and continues to weaken through Lammas; at Mabon, He is sacrificed (in His vegetable aspect, as crops are harvested). At Samhain, He becomes the Lord of the Underworld, and is reborn at Yule. Continuing to grow through Imbolc, at Ostara, He meets and impregnates the Goddess, and at Beltane He marries Her. Then, again at Litha, His Winter-self brings the battle back to defeat his Oak persona."

Other Traditions describe the God's life cycle a little differently, but in no Wiccan mythology does the God's cycle perfectly match the human cycle of birth, growth, death, and rebirth.

The Goddess's cycle is likewise hard to match to human cycles. That She gets pregnant before She's married (at least in Johnson's interpretation) fits well enough with human experience, but giving birth as a crone and then recovering Her youth is not so typical. Why don't the stages of the Gods's lives correspond better with ours? The "simple" answer is that even though we find it easiest to give the Gods humanoid forms and characteristics, They aren't for us alone.

In my Tradition's understanding, the Gods are the cycles and forces of Nature. *She* is all that is eternal and generative. In practical terms, She is the planet, its ecosystems, its weather and species, the process of evolution—and this extends beyond Earth, beyond our solar system, and beyond the Milky Way to include the whole universe and all its physics, no matter if, or when, or how well we grasp them. *He* is all that dies and is reborn. On our scale this includes plants and animals. Geophysically this includes the slowly changing features of our landscapes and the moving tectonic plates. Beyond that, this encompasses the born, dancing, and dying stars and galaxies.

The Goddess and God's relationship, which we describe in our limited terms as parent and child, and queen and consort, is the Spiral Dance. And no matter how much we act like it, our music is not the only music playing, and we humans are not the only dancers. As far as we know, though, we are the only species to know—or attempt to know—the Gods intellectually as well as intuitively.

While Jungian psychology has the disadvantage of being ever so species-centric, it can aid our understanding of the God and Goddess. Though it's an oversimplification and possibly a misapprehension of the theory, it's useful to think of the Goddess as the unconscious, and to think of the twin aspects of the God (Winter and Summer) as the light and dark—extroverted and introverted, active and contemplative—facets of our personalities. But the old literary interpretation (developed well by John and Caitlin Matthews) of Goddess as "sovereignty" and the God as aspects of stewardship are also useful analogies.

In fact, one reason that Wicca is such a serviceable religion is that its cosmology is rich with meaning on many, many levels. There's no serious proposal of supernatural deity, apart or distinct from natural process, and no need for a division between matter and spirit. The battle of the Oak and Holly Kings, played out at Yule and Litha, resolves this potential conflict satisfactorily—it *feels* right, even if it keeps our left brains guessing!

Litha, then, as celebrated with a battle between the Oak and Holly Kings, is really a moment of cooperative transition. This Sabbat celebrates the abundance of Summer's warmth and strength, and the creativity and growth it facilitates. At the same time, it recognizes the inevitability of—to put it bluntly—decay. On the other hand, by making Holly a king too, we acknowledge that "decay" is a mechanism of rebirth via death in the service of life.

In Arthurian legend, the Wounded King is wounded in "the thigh," a euphemism for "genitals." This is to say that a wounded king can't perpetuate the kingdom: He can't fertilize the land (or the queen). Therefore, he can't maintain prosperity or lineage. Whether the wound created the situation or reflected it was always ambiguous; only the analogy was clear. But in older legend, the blood of the Wounded King is the agent of fertilization. This is why, in ancient legends, the Wounded King had to be killed.

When Oak and Holly battle in Wiccan Circles, all the significant elements of legend are represented. Oak, when killed or wounded, concedes that His control over the Year has begun to wane, and that Summer's abundance will give over to Winter's fallowness. Yet Oak's death is but the prerequisite to the rebirth that will come of Winter's gestational reign, a rebirth that will ultimately and eternally mean Winter's wounding and death. There is a balance here: a rhythm of death and rebirth that makes the battle more cooperative than contentious; a rhythm that keeps the Wheel of the Year rolling.

The Oak King's crown glitters under the Summer Sun, representing the Sun itself in its round and full golden glory, and radiating all the colors of strength and growth. And even when it's knocked from the Oak King's head by the Holly King's sword, and even when Oak's Summer crown falls to the ground, it still glitters, for Litha is only mid-Summer, and not yet is Oak's reign ended. His defeat now only presages what is to come. For now, we still make merry and enjoy the generous abundance of the Summer.

ore

The contrast between the mid-Summer Sun's blazing heat and bright light with the dark ferocity of Summer thunder storms is at the heart of much Litha lore. My Druid friends tell me that there's no historical basis in their tradition for an observation of Mid-Summer, but they celebrate anyway. "Here," Kirk Thomas of Tucson's Sonoran Sunrise Grove of ADF Druids says, "we use the Gaulish pantheon and invoke Taranis, god of thunder and rain, to help bring on the monsoon season." ("Monsoons" is what southern Arizonans call the much-needed and anticipated Summer rains.)

Gamlinginn, an Asatru Priest, says a word for "Midsummer" is found in the old texts, and a mid-Summer's blot (*blot* is pronounced to rhyme with *boat*, and means "rite of blessing") is inferred from references to "special feasting" at the time of the Summer Solstice and from the appearance in the texts of a word for "Midwinter blot." Gamlinginn's essay "Concerning the Modern Asatru Calendar" doesn't specifically mention a thunder god, as our Druid source, Kirk Thomas, does, but the Asatru god Thor is surely one of the best-known thunder gods in the Western world!

The Gaulish thunder god, Taranis, was associated with Jupiter by the Romans. (Jupiter inherited the emblem of a Sun wheel from an earlier Roman Sun god, Summanus.) Lightning bolts were considered by the Romans and probably by the Celts as being actual sparks from the Sun, and lightning's association with thunder explains thunder gods' connection with mid-Summer Sun festivals.

Julius Caesar identified three Celtic gods as *Dispater*, or father of the gods. These three include a god with a hammer (who may well have been Taranis), Cernunnos, and Silvanus. Here we can see the three best-known aspects of Wicca's God: a thunderer-hammerer, perhaps an artisan god; the lord of the animals; and, possibly, a vegetation god (*silva*, sometimes spelled *sylva*, is Latin for "wood," as in a forest or grove). Taranis, the thunder god, may be "represented by the Taran of the Welsh tale of Kulwych," says J.A. MacCulloch in *The Religion of the Ancient Celts*.

In *Bulfinch's Mythology*, the tale is told as Kilwich (sometimes spelled Culhwch) and Olwen, but there's no Taranis in it. There is, however, a king (the father of Olwen, a young maiden who is beset and injured by her suitors) and a giant. The king sets Kilwich on a number of difficult tasks that the young man must accomplish before he can win Olwen's hand in marriage. The defeat of the giant is one of them.

Even if we can't place a "Taran" directly into this tale, at least not without reference to more obscure books than most of us will ever read, we can certainly understand that this is another "Oak and Holly story." There are two strong indications of this. First, in asking his cousin Arthur (yes, King Arthur) for the help he needs to find Olwen and win her hand in marriage, the knights of Camelot are allowed one year to locate the maiden. But at the end of the year, they have not found her. Thus Kilwich is frustrated in his quest; one might even say "defeated." The other clue that this much-revised tale is an Oak and Holly story is that once Olwen is found, the young solar suitor must defeat or somehow satisfy the nearly impossible standards of her father, an older king whose authority depends on his relationship to the fair maid. Taran might once have been the giant or the father of Olwen, but, in any case, as the old or "dark" solar aspect of the God, he'd have been defeated at the Summer Solstice.

This same contrast—between the young king and the old king, the bright heat and the dark storms of Summer—reminds us that the Wheel of the Year is turning, and that the kingship of the Year is turned from the Summer's Oak King to the Winter's Holly King. Oh, it's not time for Holly to ascend to the throne quite yet: According to different Traditions of Wicca, this happens at Lammas or Mabon, or Samhain, at one of the harvest festivals when the God dies in His grain and game aspects, and His more introspective aspects take over in the world and in our consciousnesses. But there's no question that Summer's days are numbered now, and that Winter's strength is growing.

Litha, with its emphasis on the Sun and on the semiannual battle between the Oak and Holly Kings, might seem like an exclusively masculine Sabbat. But, as ever, we must remember the Goddess! Mid-Summer is important to Her, too, and, of old, fertility rites were performed to ensure the "womanly abundance" of pregnancy and healthy children. In Ireland, for instance, if people didn't perform the appropriate fertility rites at the fairy queen (goddess) Aine's seat, she and her court would perform the rites themselves!

Fairies, of course, are associated more with moonlight than with sunlight. In fact, the Celtic holidays, both in Britain and on the Continent, were considered to begin at moonrise on the night before the sacred day. "The name *La Lunade* is still given to the Midsummer festival in parts of France," J.A. MacCulloch declared when he wrote *The Religion of the Ancient Celts* in 1911. These days, a more common understanding, particularly among the older Traditions of Wicca, is that the Sabbats begin at midnight, and it's still considered especially propitious when a Sabbat falls on a full Moon.

The Moon's association with tides and waters makes it reasonable to dress wells—tend them, pull weeds, repoint any stones that have been erected around them, decorate them with seasonal flowers, and bring votive offerings to them—at mid-Summer, when the Sun (the Moon's consort) is at its strongest and when the light of day lasts longest. Wells are associated with fertility, too, and, of course, a water supply is essential for the survival of any family or village. In many places, people depend on Summer floods (such as the "monsoon rains" here in Tucson) to keep the crops growing another few weeks until the harvest begins, while depending also upon those floods not being so high as to destroy homes and sweep pastures away.

At mid-Summer, then, it's important to honor the Waters that are holy to the Goddess. So important is well-tending in both Celtic and Norse cultures that neglect of it, according to legends, brings disaster upon the wardens of the wells, and sometimes upon their communities too. This is still true. Here in Tucson, for instance, a water conservation program called Beat the Peak goes into effect every Summer. At this time, we are called upon to be more mindful of our water use, for even though there are no sand dunes or camels here, this *is* a desert, and water is a precious resource.

While the preoccupation with water wells and springs is more evocative of Celts than Northern cultures, their perceptions of the horse as a divine animal are similar. J.A. MacCulloch says, "The horse was sacrificed both by Celts and Teutons at the Midsummer festival, undoubtedly as a divine animal." MacCulloch tells us that in Ireland, "...a man wearing a horse's head rushed through the fire, and was supposed to represent all cattle...." He also relates the legend of Each Labra (pronounced *ee-och*

Labra): "…a horse which lived in a mound and issued from it every Mid-summer eve to give oracles for the coming year…."

Horses are divine by virtue of their association with the Gods. Epona, represented by her totem animal, the White Horse of Uffington (an ancient carving in the chalk hills of Oxfordshire), was an important Mother Goddess for the British and the Continental Celts. For many of us, She still is. For the Asatru, the horse is associated with Freyr, an agricultural fertility god. In old Teutonic rituals in Europe, which embrace but aren't limited to the Norse heritage from which Asatru draws, a horse's head, real or carved, was burned in the mid-Summer bonfire.

The custom of sacrificing a king or surrogate symbols of royalty to ensure the fertility of the land, specifically in crops and more broadly in the general well-being of the people, is old and has gone through many revisions. One of them is instead of killing an animal to sanctify it and those it represents, one beast or many are driven between fires. In modern Wicca, this fertility rite is remembered at Beltane by some Traditions and at Litha by others. Today, of course, the sacrifice of any living creature is not part of Wiccan, Asatru, or Druid rituals, but fertility is still invoked and items of value are still offered to the Gods as part of most Neo-Pagan rituals.

For Wiccans, the offerings come in various forms. There's the effort it takes to perform a ritual, whether it is the creation and burning of a Sun wheel or the costuming and choreography of a King's Battle. There is also the sharing of Cakes and Ale, often with the words, "As the Gods share with us, so we share with Them." In some mid-Summer rites, there are other "sacrifices" as well (see the section about Litha rituals).

But lest we forget this, even informal rituals can honor Wicca's cosmology, and this is because Wicca is a religion of experience. Wicca is a Nature Religion, yes, but the Elements are with us in our city lives too. It doesn't even take much to notice them, especially not at Litha, and to understand that we are blessed by each of them in virtually every aspect of our lives. It's not proselytizing to share these observations with our non-Pagan friends either, because what is for us a religious reality is for everyone else a material reality, and one most people find satisfying to notice and appreciate—especially in the Summer.

Rituals

It's quite common to celebrate Litha with a King's Battle, mirroring the one at Yule. At Litha, though, the Holly King wins, because from the Summer Solstice onward, the Wheel turns toward Winter. As appropriate and as much fun a King's Battle is, though, it's not the only way Wiccans celebrate. Another way is with a blazing Sun wheel, like the ones Asatruar are likely to use.

Directions for making a Sun wheel can be found on page 81. Here, I'll just say that you need to be careful when you put Fire in motion in your rituals. It wouldn't be a bad idea to make two wheels and practice with one before you light the other in Circle. You can use a kiddie wading pool to receive the wheel. The pool of water—make that "capital-*W*" Water—represents the womb of the Goddess, to which we all return when we die. One way the Sun wheel is symbolic of the God is that its blazing glory ends with its return to the grave-that-is-a-womb. After all, in our experience, Fire and Water, as Sun and rain, work together to make the Earth fertile.

If burning a Sun wheel is not possible in your circumstances, you can make its creation part of the Litha ritual and simply cover it with a blue cloth, representing the immersion of its "flames" in "water." Another option is to use a Sun-shaped or brightly colored star-shaped piñata. While these can be set on fire and dropped into water, too, an alternative is to fill it with candy and break it open to symbolize the abundance that comes from the Sun's strength and the harvest to come. The following "Sun Wheel Rite" can be performed with any of these options.

Sun Wheel Rite

In a Circle cast as usual for yourself or your group, introduce the Sun Wheel Rite like this:

The Sun is bright and blazing now,
a-flaming in the sky,
And yet we know that like all days,
this one will soon go by.
Though kingly now, and fiery strong,
toward Winter He shall fade,
This day, the Sun we honor,
with a blazing accolade!
With Wheel as dazzling as the Sun,
with turning brave and true,
We celebrate abundance,
and salute the fiery hue!
We honor now the death He'll die,
as the Wheel turns toward the West,
And honor too the waters
of the womb-grave where He'll rest.
All hail! the Sun, all hail! His strength,
on this, His longest day:
All hail! His passing and rebirth—all hail!
His glorious rays!

If creating the Sun wheel or Sun piñata (see page 83) is part of your ritual, you'll already have the necessary materials in the Circle. Bring them forth at this time and set to its construction. Apart from necessary instructions and requests to pass the scissors or glue, comments should be restricted to encouragement and reassurance of the Sun God as He enjoys His glory in full awareness that His death is just a few short months away.

When the Sun wheel or piñata is finished, or if it has been brought ready-made into the Circle, consecrate and bless it with these words, or in a similar way if you prefer to write your own lines:

You form of Sun, all bright of rays,
Blessed be on this longest of days!
We hold you holy, named as Fire,
as the God's life and desire!
Blessed be as sacred spark,
and on Your journey now embark!

You may further wish to offer the consecrated wheel or piñata words of blessing and appreciation such as these:

Hail, O Sun, from first of May,
we've enjoyed each Summer's day!

or

Go Sun, go Sun, you've had a good run
across the skies—and you're still not done!

These can be as silly or as serious as you're inclined, for as the Goddess charges, mirth and reverence should always be with us.

When the wheel or piñata has been consecrated and blessed, it's time to organize your enactment of the turning of the Wheel. If you're planning to light it and guide or carry it into a body of water (a wading pool or a giant caldron or other container, for example), make sure that there are Wardens ready and equipped to handle any emergencies, and make sure the children have a clear view from a safe distance.

The same cautions apply if a flaming wheel is being carried around the Circle on a fireproof axle. Beware of sudden gusts of wind, and be prepared to stop, drop, and roll the wheel rather than risk injury to anyone. You can always relight it again when it's directly over the Water. The Gods will not be offended by your erring on the side of caution. Instead, They will appreciate your having the gumption to give it a go!

When the blazing Sun wheel or piñata has reached the Water, or the non-blazing Sun piñata has been whacked sufficiently, or the non-blazing wheel has been covered to symbolize Summer's ceding of the Year to Winter, it's time to recognize that the God, in His solar aspect, is now past His prime. Though still strong with authority, still generous with warmth and light for many weeks to come, He's beyond His zenith. Acknowledge this with these words, or similar words of your own:

O Sun, your light surrounds us still; your warmth, luxurious, remains.
Not for many a late-Summer's week will we feel the Autumn's cool constrains.
Yet at Solstice we behold—yea, the Wheel of the Year has rolled;
now has Summer's bell been tolled, and Winter subtly foretold.
We hail You, Sun, and settle now to spend with You remaining days
in present joy, in memory grand, and confident of rebirth's ways.

Now, if there are any flames still burning or any representations of the Sun still dry or visible, extinguish them, submerge them, or cover them, respectively. When you proceed to Cakes and Ale, toast the Sun, talk about your plans for the rest of the Summer (maybe think about a coven or family picnic, or maybe a trip to a beach or amusement park, if you haven't enjoyed one yet this year), and then close the Circle as you usually do.

If you haven't got a "usual way" of casting and closing a Circle, please refer to Appendix A of this book's companion volume, *Celebrating the Seasons of Life: Samhain to Ostara*. (Appendix A of this book offers a few suggestions for setting up your Circle indoors, in case you don't have an outdoor space where you can comfortably work.)

This ritual, on a smaller scale, can be performed by a solitary Wiccan. The modifications are easy to make: Use a round pan of water and a small Sun wheel with an unwound coat hanger for an axle. If necessary, perform it in the bathroom over the tub—you could even be *in* the tub and skyclad! Thanks to the popularity of home spas, burning candles in the bathroom is not such a peculiar idea anymore, and if your ritual needs to be disguised, it can pass for an admittedly eccentric personal ritual.

If you want to celebrate the Solstice with a more secular ritual so the children present can be more exuberant or so non-Pagans can be involved, another option is to perform a Sun Circle, which is described in the next rite. You can even call it an "activity" or a "game" instead of a ritual, yet it quite directly symbolizes the turning of the seasons.

Summer Solstice Rite

Everyone should dress brightly in yellow, red, or orange. If anyone wants to wear garlands or ribbons in their hair, so much the better. Any food you provide should be Sun-colored, and perhaps round. In fact, why not make it a potluck and ask everyone to bring Sun-colored or Summer-colored food! (The list of these is long. It includes various melons and berries, chips and salsa, pizza, and cookies.)

Gather (outside is best, but inside is fine) and join hands, forming a circle. The group leader should give a brief explanation of the Summer Solstice, emphasizing, if necessary, that it's an astronomical event—something that scientists measure. The fact that American calendars call it the beginning of Summer, while in other places it's recognized as mid-Summer, can be a cultural tidbit if presenting it as religious would offend anyone.

Calling the Quarters in a secular circle needs to be subtle. Wiccans usually hail the Watchtowers, but it's equally respectful to acknowledge the Elements in other ways. For example, you can suggest that before the group "plays the game," "learns the song," or "tries the dance," everyone should think about the many ways they each enjoy Summer.

In honor of East, you might say, "We sure appreciate Summer breezes...and the air-conditioning sometimes!" Perhaps, unwittingly, everyone honors South when they enjoy the extra hours of daylight that Summer affords us. And even if we do like the air-conditioning sometimes, the warmth of Summer is a comforting memory when Winter lies in heaps on the ground, as it does in many places. West? Well, lots of people have a favorite swimmin' hole or like a run through the sprinkler. Or how about a cool shower after a hot day at work? Not to mention, plenty of us feel refreshed after a Summer rain. And don't forget the cool drinks! North? Oh, shade, glorious shade! What about tree houses or decks? Every season brings with it the blessings of all the Elements, and Summer is no exception. Very few people, even among non-Pagans, can object to appreciating those blessings, which we can just as well call "saluting those Summer pleasures."

If this were an openly Wiccan ritual, once you recognized the presence of the Elements and their blessings, you would then invoke the Gods. If that's not something you can do overtly, do it this way: Take a moment to express how much you care for the people gathered with you. If it's a small group, address everyone personally. If it's a bigger group or if people would be embarrassed by personal praise, just acknowledge that everyone's friendship is terribly important to you, that people standing by each other and enjoying each other's company and growth is rare and beautiful, and that you're all lucky to be "in each other's circle." Because, as initiated Wiccans know, each of us is God and Goddess, calling upon everyone's own best self *is* an invocation.

Now, perhaps with a little squeeze of hands going around the circle, you can get down to the "party" part of this informal ritual. To the tune of "Row, Row, Row Your Boat," sing this song (and yes, you can sing it as a round if anyone wants to):

The Sun's high in the sky, Summer's halfway through,
But it'll still be light and warm another month or two!
The Sun is moving south again, Autumn's on the way,
But the Sun's still bright and strong on this Solstice Day!

You can dance to the song too: Step deosil (clockwise) on the first, second, and fourth lines, and step widdershins (counterclockwise) on the third. Or to make it easier for anyone unable to move like this, bring your arms up slowly on the first and second lines, lower them on the third, and raise them up again in a hurrah gesture on the fourth line. If you're singing the song as a round, you can get a "wave" effect if half the circle sings the first two lines while the other half sings the second two.

When you're done with your Sun-Circle dance, you can "close" by reiterating how meaningful your friendships are, and how fine it is that you are not only there for each other when things get serious, but you also have so much fun together. Our relationships are made of the mirth and reverence that the Goddess charges us to make part of our lives, and we honor Her in keeping Her *Charge*, no matter how little like a Circle our circles look.

You can relate the Elemental blessings to the feast you're about to share too. If you're feasting inside, the *Air*-conditioning feels good after your dance. If you're feasting outside, perhaps there's a breeze you'll enjoy, or you can offer people paper fans to cool themselves with. Is some of the food spicy, or *Fire*-y? Do you all have a bit of color in your cheeks from your dancing and singing? Will there be *Water*melon? Cool drinks? Is there a wading pool for people to dangle their feet in? Do you live where there's a swimming pool people can enjoy? Will you be enjoying *North*-ern shade? Perhaps you'll be lounging on soft but sturdy (wooden? metal? cotton upholstered or cushioned?) furniture, indoors or out. Taking pleasure in any of these things is a respectful response to the Elements.

A group hug after your Sun Circle will help ground everyone, and so will eating. Although it may not be quite as obvious (and it takes longer), a potluck feast is symbolically the same as sharing Cakes and Ale in a formally cast Circle. And, thus, what seems like a playful Summer afternoon to non-Pagans can serve as a ritual for Wiccan participants!

In the old days, it's not likely that mid-Summer rituals were significantly different from Beltane rituals. A bonfire was central to the celebration, and sometimes a "Summerpole" was erected and decorated with flowers and leafy branches. A deosil (sunwise) dance around a fire or a pole was, probably—or so folklorists at the turn of the 20th century believed—accompanied by chanting and songs of praise for the Sun God. "The livelier the dance the better would be the harvest," J.A. MacCulloch remarks in *The Religion of the Ancient Celts*.

Nowadays, not so many of us grow our own crops, and few Wiccans have cattle or other domestic livestock to drive between two fires to ensure their fertility. Often as not, our Litha rites involve the reenactment of the battle of Oak and Holly or the display of a burning Sun wheel. Yet, there are ways to recall even older, less sophisticated celebrations. The Sunpole Rite is one.

The Sunpole Rite

This ritual combines Beltane's dance with more vivid symbols of mid-Summer. It also includes aspects of a ritual devised for a community rite that took place in Tucson many years ago, which is still well-remembered. You'll need some red and some gold tinsel garlands (the red *and* gold ones are good too), and a pole with a stand. You can use an old Yule tree stem, a 10-foot long dowel, or even a 10-foot length of PVC pipe. You'll also need a length of ribbon or a leather thong long enough to wind around the pole two or three times and then tie, and a pair of scissors.

Tie one end of several garlands to a metal ring just a little larger than the diameter of your pole, and then slide the ring over the top end of the pole. (We use a "Christmas tree" stand to hold our Maypoles and our Sunpoles.)

Not all of us have an outdoor or indoor space big enough to set up a 10-foot tall pole and dance around it. If you don't, not to worry: Use a staff and ask someone to hold it up at the center of your Circle. This means that either you'll have to be a little more careful as you dance, or you'll have to promise to extricate the poor soul in the middle when you're done!

At Beltane, our circles around the pole make a braid, for we're dancing the sacred marriage of the Goddess and God. At Litha, dancing the

Sunpole, we can do the same thing, but we can also circle the pole in the same direction, just winding the garlands around the pole—not too tightly around anyone holding it! The point here isn't to symbolize a marriage, but to honor and encourage the strength and brightness of the Sun.

An idea to enrich this rite was inspired by Sue Bond, a Tucson Priestess. As you take up the garland you will dance with, offer to it (to the Sun God through it) some part of the abundance of your life. Lady Sue, who showed us this way of giving back to the Gods, is the mother of two children. As I recall, her offering (to the garland, to the pole, to the God) was some of the patience she'd learned from motherhood. Other blessings mentioned that year included the generosity of friends, good fortune, the joy of travel, the pleasure of living somewhere warm, the blessings of a good marriage, and delight in the sound of surf breaking upon the shore.

Outside, the physical Sun will make the garlands seem to sparkle and twinkle. Inside, you can use flashlights to achieve a similar effect. This is particularly appropriate if you're including children, because kids love to wave flashlights around, and they aren't very often invited to do so! As you carry the garlands around the pole, wrapping it in the brightness of the mid-Summer Sun, you can take your pick of chants.

"We all die like the Sun God" is fine, but if you'd rather avoid the overt reference to His inevitable death, even though it does facilitate the rebirth we rejoice in, try what I call the "God chant." It's a companion to the "Goddess chant," or the "Isis, Astarte" chant that comes from the beloved chorus of an old Charlie Murphy song. I don't know who wrote the God's version, but Tucson's "camping contingent" has known it for many years now. To the same tune and rhythm as the "Isis, Astarte," it goes like this:

> *Odin, Cernunnos, Merlin, Coyote, Osiris, Shiva…Horned One!*
> (*Coyote* is pronounced **Coy-yo-tay**, and *Shiva* has almost two syllables.)

You may want to make up your own chants to the Sun, and if there are enough people to sing two or more chants in a round, this would be a particularly nice offering to make to the Gods.

When you've wound the garlands around the pole, tie them off with the ribbon or leather, leaving at least 6 inches of garland at the end of the pole for people to cut off pieces to take home. If the lengths you cut off are long enough, you can tie them into circlets and wear them as crowns until the ritual has ended—or for a longer time than that, if you like!

Wiccans and other Neo-Pagans should do this ritual as part of a regularly cast Circle; with non-Pagans, just do it! Although most Wiccans follow essentially the same Order of Circle in their rites, Traditions do differ as to whether the celebration or magic should be done before or after the rite of Cakes and Ale. The decision rests largely on whether the Tradition calls for fasting or not: Traditions that *do* fast tend to celebrate their feast before they do the Work of the Circle, and Traditions that *don't* fast tend to consecrate and share Cakes and Ale after celebrating or working magic. If you're a solitary or a coven unaffiliated with a distinct Tradition, you can make this decision for yourself on any basis that seems reasonable to you.

Here are invocations of the Gods written specially for a Litha rite that celebrates mid-Summer with a Sunpole. You can use these as they are, or modify them to suit you:

Goddess Earth, warmed by the Sun,
basking in the Summer's light,
Join us as this rite's begun,
Your heart with us while the days are bright!

God of Life and of Rebirth,
Light the lover, Light the son
Here to honor Your great worth,
we invoke You, oh Bright One!

As you prepare to dance around the pole, you might introduce the dance like this:

These garlands each a Sun's bright ray;
we are the lives on which they beam;
We dance for joy on this longest day,
and energize the God's great gleam.
As the pole we circle round,
so the Sun goes 'round the Year,
As His light shines to the ground,
so our lives are warmed with cheer.

On this day our garland-beams
wind deosil unto the ground,
So our Lord dies, so it seems,
but His rebirth from death comes round.
Brightly shining in the sky,
brightly burning in our hearts,
We share the knowing in His eye,
and love and trust Him by our arts.

If you can arrange drumming or clapping to accompany your chanting, so much the better. If that's not feasible, maybe you can wear bells on your wrists or ankles. Holding the garland with one hand, you might also hold a bell or bells, a tambourine, a maraca, or a similar instrument in the other while you dance.

Once you've wound the Sunpole with the garlands, finish the line of the chant you are in the middle of, and then pause for a moment, perhaps filling the air with one last rattle or jingle of your instruments. Another way to earth your energy now is to shout a single word to represent the abundance you've shared in dancing the pole: *patience, generosity, luck, love,* and *vacation.* In these times, words reflecting our blessings might also include *employment, housing,* and *insurance.*

To thank the Gods as you close your Circle, you might say something like this:

Lord of Light, Lord of the Dance,
Lord of the turning Year's romance,
Welcome You have been today;
now go if You must, and if You will, stay!

Mother Goddess, charming Earth,
You through whom we know rebirth,
Welcome You have been today;
now go if You must, and if You will, stay!

I haven't included Quarter calls or dismissals. It's not necessary to customize them for each Sabbat: Many Wiccans who do use new or season-tailored invocations of the Gods at each Sabbat prefer to balance that variety by calling the Quarters the same way in every Circle. This is the way of my Tradition, and was always the choice of my coven. However, if you want

Sabbat-specific Quarter calls and dismissals, here are some that you can make specific to each Sabbat while also enjoying the reliability of repetition in each Circle:

Calls

Glad come to _____, Guardians,
'Towers of East, this Circle ward.
Now as our ritual does begin,
sound to us your Airy chord.

Glad come to _____, Guardians,
'Towers of South, this Circle ward.
Now as our ritual does begin,
warm us with passion all amoured.

Glad come to_____, Guardians,
'Towers of West, this Circle ward.
Now as our ritual does begin,
bring intuition and concord.

Glad come to _____, Guardians,
'Towers of North, this Circle ward.
Now as our ritual does begin,
Ground us, and our rites record.

Dismissals

Glad part from _____, Guardians,
'Towers of East, hail and farewell!
With thanks for your voice, in
  honor we send
You back to the Quarter where
  you dwell.

Glad part from _____, Guardians,
'Towers of South, hail and farewell!
With thanks for your fervor, in
  honor we send
You back to the Quarter where
  you dwell.

Glad part from _____, Guardians,
'Towers of West, hail and farewell!
With thanks for your heart, in
  honor we send
You back to the Quarter where you
  dwell.

Glad part from _____, Guardians,
'Towers of North, hail and farewell!
With thanks for your fixity, in honor
  we send
You back to the Quarter where you
  dwell.

Consecrating Sunscreen

At Litha, it's warm enough in most places in the Northern Hemisphere to conduct our rituals outside, and that puts us in danger of sunburn. "Nor do I ask aught of sacrifice," the Goddess assures us in the *Charge*, and this includes burnt offerings. Therefore, it's wise to use sunscreen.

I've heard the objection that sunscreen ought not to be worn in a Circle because it hasn't been consecrated. Consecrations of such mundane substances aren't included in many Books of Shadows, and too many of us ignore the challenge to create one. Well, I live in Arizona, and Canyondancer has had a few cancerous spots removed from his face and arms, so we always keep sunscreen within our reach. Here's a happy way, mirthful yet effective, to consecrate sunscreen so as not to offend the Gods or clergy by wearing it into any Tradition's Circle.

A Consecration for Sunscreen

No sacrifice, burnt offerings none,
nor shall we cower from the Sun.
To Circle we do not go mundane,
yet would protect our fair membrane.
Therefore, by Earth, this oil I make
sacred for protection's sake.
Therefore, by Air, this liquid balm
be seen as sacred, in my palm.
Therefore, by Fire, to fire command,
this lotion is blessed by my hand.
Therefore, by Water, this watery substance be
blessed and applied all over me.
In spirit nor flesh, thanks to this consecration,
this rite won't end with my conflagration.
By Goddess and God, by even and odd,
by mirth and reverence, by rhyme and sense,
blessed be this sunscreen here,
so I go into Circle with no sunburn fear.

Litha Vow

At mid-Summer, the memory of Winter's paralyzing cold is distant. When there's no snow on the ground, it's hard to worry about having enough wood or heating oil to keep our houses warm. During the Summer months, Nature's abundance eases some of our financial burdens: Less money is spent at grocery stores because we, or our friends, have gardens that provide well for us—given we like tomatoes and zucchini! While Samhain is when many Wiccans invite the family ghosts to visit, Litha is when reunions with our living family members often take place. Also, there is no pressure to give gifts at Litha, which you might feel at Yule. Instead, Litha is the time to give of ourselves physically by walking and playing with each other. At the same time Nature is maturing, our inner children are freest to generate their special energy. Huzzah for that!

Take Litha's vow each time you accomplish something on your Summer to do list, whether it's organizing your closets or sticking with that early-morning running program for a whole month. All these things will contribute to the harvest that will sustain you next Winter, and they'll all make memories that will brighten your dark Winter days:

Mid-Summer is come on the Wheel of the Year!
With warmth we are sensual; long days are our cheer.
The Sun's at His strongest, though soon He shall fade:
I'll engage the abundance, and still love the shade.
The present is plenty, and plenty is real
enough to light up the dark side of the Wheel.
I vow love and trust in the God of long light,
and to wave His bright sword 'gainst all fears of the night.

ctivities

At Litha, our rituals honor the Sun and the height of its strength. One way Wiccans do this is with a Sun wheel. You can make one ahead of time, or you can make one as part of your ritual. Here's one way to create a Sun wheel.

Paper Sun Wheel

Shaded by a patio roof, O'Gaea holds a paper Sun wheel made of poster board, wrapping paper, tissue paper, and curling ribbon.

You will need two pieces of poster board—choose red, orange, yellow, or gold. You will also need at least one empty toilet paper roll, scissors, craft glue or tape, and some decorative scraps: pink, red, gold, or orange curling ribbon, tissue paper, glitter, and perhaps some red or gold doilies. You may think of other decorations to include too.

Before you start constructing your wheel, determine where you will be holding your ritual. You may need to make a smaller wheel depending on the size of your ritual space. Also, remember that no matter how big your Sun wheel is, and whether or not you can really set it on fire, it can still be brilliantly colored and brightly shiny. Its spirit can be as big as your love of the God.

First, cut a circle from each piece of poster board. (Make sure they are the same size.) Next, take your empty toilet paper roll and cut it in half, lengthwise. Then cut each half into 1-inch pieces. (You will attach these between the circles in order to give the wheel some dimension.) Glue the toilet paper roll pieces to one circle first, and let the glue dry before attaching the second circle. (If you're doing this project as part of your ritual, it'll be quicker to use tape instead of glue.)

Next, decorate both sides of the wheel with doilies, scraps of tissue paper, curled ribbons, glitter, and anything else that is bright and shiny. Gold foil or prismatic wrapping paper make a nice touch, too, especially if your ritual will be held outside.

Whether you're going to burn the Sun wheel or not, you'll be consecrating it and offering it blessings in return for those we enjoy from the Sun God. You'll also be offering it encouragement—a bit of a pep talk, if you will—and assurances that you remember the early days of Summer, that you'll continue to appreciate the Sun even as it fades in the skies with Winter's approach, and that you anticipate its rebirth at Yule. At each Sabbat, we acknowledge that the Wheel ever turns, and even as we savor each Sabbat moment, we're aware of those past and those yet to come.

Part of the "craft" in Witchcraft is practical. For some Sabbat celebrations, a bit of down-home "engineering" is required. For instance, rigging a flaming Sun wheel to roll into a wading pool is tricky. Ideally, you will be able to use a natural grassy slope, perhaps a small dirt hill in your yard. From my experience, the easiest way to accomplish this is to make a ramp, the same as children sometimes make for their bikes or skateboards.

You can make a ramp out of wood or cardboard, but you must keep the wheel rolling fast enough so as not to ignite it. (Keep a fire extinguisher nearby in case of an emergency.) Probably the safest option is to ask two adults to carry the burning wheel on an axle made of unwound metal coat hangers. (Make a pencil-sized hole through the center of the wheel and insert the axel. Have an adult stand on either side of the wheel and hold an end of the axel in order to carry it to the water. With the wheel in the middle, the flames should be at a safe distance from the people carrying it.) Depending on how quickly the wheel burns, there might be time to make a circuit around your Circle before it's lowered into the wading pool. If your wheel is small enough, another option is to lower it into a giant plastic cauldron filled with water.

You may think of alternatives as you prepare for your ritual. Whatever you do, be very careful with fire and do not try anything foolish. Remember, She asks naught of sacrifice: Wiccans are *not* into burnt offerings! If all else seems impractical for any reason, make a one-sided Sun wheel and burn a tea light on it, extinguishing it with water from the altar at the appropriate point in your ritual.

Sun Piñata

If you're not inclined or don't have a safe place to celebrate Litha with a flaming Sun wheel, try using a Sun piñata instead. In my corner of the world, there is a wide variety of piñatas for sale in party stores and grocery stores. If you don't find any ready-made piñatas where you live, they are relatively easy to put together. In addition to the piñata, you'll need a blindfold and a lightweight stick. (A yardstick is fine to use. You can make it more festive by wrapping it in colorful tissue paper.)

To make your own piñata, you can go the elaborate route of blowing up a balloon and covering it with papier-mâché, taking care not to make the papier-mâché so thick that it will be hard to break. Once the papier-mâché is dry, insert a needle to pop the balloon. You can cut a hole in the bottom and insert some treats, using tape to cover the hole so that they don't fall out before the piñata is broken. Another option (the easier route) is to use a paper grocery bag as your piñata. Either way, decorate your Sun piñata with rows of crumpled or fringed tissue paper. (Cut strips of tissue paper 2-inches wide, and then cut 1 inch of fringe into each strip. Glue the solid inch directly onto the piñata, layering the rows of fringe just as you would layer shingles on your roof). Fill the piñata with candy or inexpensive toys. Or, if the ritual is for grown-ups, fill it with blessings written on Sun-colored squares of paper. Suspend the piñata on a string from a ceiling or tree branch, for example, and use a lightweight stick to break or tear it. Take turns swinging at it until it falls apart, releasing the goodies inside. The person swinging the stick should be blindfolded, of course, and the number of swings each person can take is usually limited to five or six, or the first person up would be the only person to have a chance of breaking the piñata!

Remember, you have to be careful when celebrating with a piñata. Make sure when you are swinging the stick, everybody is out of the way! Injuries are not common, but they're possible. They can really spoil an otherwise wonderful time, so make sure everyone is standing at a safe distance from the person swinging.

Camping

A VW camper's awning is extended by a tarp to
provide cover for firewood during our camping trip.

The outdoor life is not for everyone, but even if you're one of the people the outdoor life isn't for, it's a nice gesture to make an effort to go at least once a year. And if it's going to be a once-a-year activity, Litha is the best time: The weather is usually good during this season, even in those places that get hearty Summer rains. Fortunately, there are ways for the inexperienced (and unenthused) to have a good time, and there are a number of alternatives to the traditional idea people have regarding camping.

The easiest way and place to camp is in your own backyard. If you've got lovely, soft grass, all you will need is some old bed linens (grass stains don't always come out), some rope, and a couple of blankets. Use the rope to string the blankets from trees, porch posts, or fences to make a tent. If you're really ambitious and the laws of your town allow you to, dig a fire pit in your lawn, line the circle with stones, and, with fallen branches from your own trees, make yourself a little fire to toast hotdogs and marshmallows. If you have a barbecue, use that. It's even okay to go inside to use the toilet and to brush your teeth. But to make it camping, give up the TV and the video games, and eat and sleep outside. (You can do the same thing in your living room if you want to. Sleep under the dining-room table, or make your rope-and-blanket tent indoors.)

Do you feel silly sleeping under the dining-room table and you don't have a suitable backyard? Try camping in a state park. We're awfully lucky here in Tucson to have a state park just a few miles north of town. Because it's on the desert floor, the temperature at Litha is hotter than we would like it to be. Even so, we have stayed overnight and celebrated a couple of Litha rites there. Places that are hot and short on shade during the day tend to be balmy at night, affording a beautiful view of the Summer sky.

Some outdoor supply shops rent equipment, and so do some universities if you have an affiliation with them. When no rain is expected on your trip, a tent—used or new—will do just fine. (You have to be careful about leaks!) Or you can rent a camper—anything from a VW bus to a full-fledged motor home. If you have an SUV, you can fold the seats in the back down and sleep there.

If you are allowed to make a campfire, you can heat water for coffee, tea, oatmeal, cider, or hot chocolate. With a grill to go over the fire, you can heat a pan of any canned food, and, of course, beef or fish steaks. You can make what we grew up calling potatoes O'Brien: potatoes cut into 1-inch (or slightly smaller) cubes, wrapped loosely in tinfoil with bits of onion and green pepper, and then cooked in the coals. Corn on the cob also cooks nicely the same way. Trust me, you won't starve when you are camping.

There are some rules to follow, of course, wherever you're camping. Don't leave food out in the open when you're done preparing and eating it. Don't leave coolers accessible either: Put them in the trunk of your car where they're not visible. It may be funny when cute forest beasties steal your food if you're camped with other people who can resupply you, but it's not so funny if that was all you had to eat for dinner. Don't be heroic and try to save your food from even small beasts, either. Okay, maybe you can chase off a chipmunk or a squirrel, but foxes, skunks, and raccoons—well, let them win. Even if they're not rabid, they bite fast and hard. Plus, She asks naught of sacrifice. (You're not "sacrificing" your food; you're sharing with the Gods, whose proxies the beasties are.)

Didn't mean to scare you there: We've been camping here in Arizona for a couple of decades now, and only twice have we seen food stolen. Once, it was a coatimundi (an animal sort of like a long, thin raccoon) that cleverly opened a cooler and took steak and chips, and once it was a skunk that was practically invited by a bowl of birdseed left beside a tent that was meant for our friends' macaw. We've seen robins and jays and some other really neat birds (one or two places we like to camp are world-renowned birding areas). We've seen chipmunks, squirrels, coatis, raccoons, skunks, and deer, but never bear (even though they live in some of the areas where we camp) or wildcats. From my experience, wild creatures may want to eat your food, but they don't usually want to eat you: As long as they hear you coming, they will usually keep out of your way. Even so, it is good to use caution and common sense in regard to animals when camping in the wild.

What can you do if you're camping in a park? If you have children, enjoy their delight in poking in the dirt, chasing birds, or climbing rocks and trees. (Yes, they might get dirty, but dirt washes off.) If there's water, you can skip stones across it, build rafts with pinecones and twigs, wade, or build dams. If there is no water, you can try building stone castles, count how many different flowers there are in bloom, make a whistle with a blade of grass held between your thumbs, see if any of the big trees are ponderosa pines (they will smell of vanilla if they are), build twig castles, listen for and mimic bird calls, see how many different animals or plants you can identify (a book from Roger Tory Peterson's *Field Guides* series [Houghton Mifflin Company] is wonderful to have with you), or look for animal tracks and try to identify them. You can also just sit quietly in camp, breathing slowly, relaxing and making yourself receptive to the manifestations of the God and Goddess: warm sunlight, gentle breezes, the sounds of the woods alive, the scent of the grasses and trees, the hum and shimmer of insects, and the magical light-and-shadow shows through branches and clouds.

Anyway, working up the courage to camp, sorting out what you'll need and where to find it, planning a couple of meals so you don't take way too much food, finding a place close to where you live—if it takes some time and energy, then consider that to be a suitable offering to the Gods. Most of us offer Them a bite of Cakes and a splash of Ale in our ritual Circles, and maybe we put a lot into making altar gear and writing invocations and all, but really, we owe Them more than that. And if, as many initiation rites tell us, we are God and Goddess, then we owe ourselves more than that too.

I'm not saying that making Tools and writing ritual isn't challenging and legitimate work—of course it is. I've labored hours over spells, and I've put my share of time and energy into my coven's Sabbats and Esbats. But I am saying that none of that is enough. Wicca, as you've heard and maybe said, is "more than a religion; it's a way of life." And that means that we have to give Wicca and its worldview, the Gods and all that we call holy, energy from the life we live outside the Circle too.

Wicca is also, I'm sure you've heard it said, a religion of experience. A lot of us will tell you that there's only so much you can learn from any book, and that, eventually, to be a Wiccan, you have to do Wicca. You must cast Circles, celebrate Sabbats and Esbats, and attune yourself to natural cycles and make them meaningful, literally and figuratively, in your everyday life. Yet another way to describe Wicca is as a Nature Religion, which means that we look to the natural world to see what's right and holy.

When you integrate those concepts, you realize (I hope) that it's necessary to go beyond learning about Nature in books. This means you have to get out in it once in a while. Maybe you really, really can't manage camping—ever. So what else can you do to put yourself in contact with the God and Goddess on a physical level? How else can you get in touch with the Earth and what lives upon it, and the cycles of seasons that all lives go through?

Obviously, I like to camp. It is one of my favorite activities throughout the Summer months. Here in Arizona, we're inclined to head for the mountains because it is cooler up there than it is down here on the desert floor. Still, for various reasons, there are a fair number of Wiccans who can't or don't want to camp. You might be one of them, but that's no reason you can't enjoy some of our favorite camping activities. And don't worry, I'm *not* talking about sleeping under the dining-room table!

Toasting Things

Now, don't get too excited: We're only talking about hotdogs and marshmallows here! But whether you build a fire indoors, which can be both cozy and appropriate if you get Summer storms around Litha, or outside by using your trusty barbecue, you can toast weenies and marshmallows at home just as well as you could in the "woo-ids."

You can even try making s'mores. All you need are graham crackers, some squares of chocolate, and marshmallows. Set a square of chocolate on a graham cracker, put it close enough to the fire to melt the chocolate a bit, top it with a toasted marshmallow, and sandwich everything with another graham cracker. And don't tell anybody I said so, but if you're at home, you can give the chocolate a head start in the microwave.

Sing-Alongs

Sing-alongs may be cornier in your home than they are in the woods when you are camping, but never mind; have a good time anyway. Around our campfires, we've relearned old scouting songs, enjoyed some newly filked words to old favorite tunes (filking is, essentially, parodying), and gotten used to some obscure old ballads. If you have children, they'll enjoy singing around a "campfire" even if you are using a fireplace or one of those short-legged, portable barbecues you can buy at hardware and home improvement stores. (I recommend those little close-to-the-ground sets because you really do lose a lot of the effect when you're standing up around a conventional barbecue.)

Here's an old song with new lyrics that most kids will enjoy (you know the tune):

> *If you're Pagan and you know it, clap your hands;*
> *If you're Pagan and you know it, clap your hands!*
> *If you're Pagan and you know it, then you really oughta show it:*
> *If you're Pagan and you know it, clap your hands!*

This is what's known as a "zipper song," because you can "zip" alternate words into it in every verse while keeping the same format. So your next lines might be: "If you're Pagan and you know it, stamp your feet" or "If you're Pagan and you know it, shout 'Huzzah!'" You and your kids will think of other actions to zip into these verses, and if your sing-along turns into a giggle-fest, so much the better!

We have also enjoyed personalizing the verses to another filked song. We call this "What Do You Do With a Drunken Wiccan?" I almost didn't include this example here because I don't want to be misunderstood as approving of drunkenness. But this old sea-chantey tune sounds great, offers many opportunities for harmonies, and can be sung as a little bit of a round if you add the "way, hey, and up she rises" lines. In fact, the verses our campers sing would probably go a long way to reforming a drunken Pagan!

> *What do you do with a drunken Wiccan?*
> *What do you do with a drunken Wiccan?*
> *What do you do with a drunken Wiccan,*
> > *Early in the morning?*

If you're adding the "way, hey, and up she rises" lines, sing them here. And to answer the question of what you do with a drunken Wiccan (or Druid or Viking), use one of the lines below or let your own experience inspire you:

> *Put him in a tent with his High Priestess…*
> *Let the babies serenade him…*
> *Lock him in the one-hole outhouse…*
> *Serenade him with the bagpipes…*
> *Introduce him to the ranger…*
> *Tie him to the Maypole till he's sober…*

Every group that sings a song like this will be able to add verses that refer to their experiences together. (No, we've never tied anyone to our Maypole, nor have we locked anyone in an outhouse. We have availed ourselves of most of the other options, though). A sing-along is a bonding experience, and it can be a lot of fun. Lullabies and oldies are other campfire favorites, too, and they might be more appropriate if you have close neighbors.

Beyond Camping

At Litha, one of the Year's two Solstices, attending a planetarium show is fine, but it's kind of bookish, even though it is three-dimensional and you are in a building with other people. Go beyond that: Get yourself a sky chart and go out and look at the stars. Figure out which constellations you're looking at. If there's a telescope shop where you live, they probably host stargazing evenings during the Summer months. Call them up, find out when they will have one, and go. Take the kids. Even in the dark, you can see their faces light up as they see a distant part of the solar system up close and personal.

During the day, within a week of the Sabbat, try going to the zoo, sailing toy or paper boats on a pond in the park, or wandering through an open-air market or street fair. When you meet other people, be cheerful, hopeful, and aware of what aspect of the Goddess and God they're showing you. Beauty? Diversity? Mirth? Be aware, too, of what aspect of the Goddess and God you're displaying to the rest of the world, and what part of Litha's bounty and divine generosity you're offering back to the Gods.

Litha Recipes

We like the food at our Litha feasts to be Sun-like: red, orange, or yellow, and round. It might be spicy too. The color connection is obvious, and so is the correspondence of spicy food with Summer heat. In fact, eating spicy food when it's hot outside can help you cool off, because it inspires perspiration.

Easy Choices

For many people, pizza is a favorite, although making it at home does heat the house if you're using the oven instead of the microwave. We don't eat pizza very often in my house: We love cheese, but it's too fatty for our arteries. We do break our diet for Sabbats, though, so sometimes we do have a big ol' sunny-colored pizza for Litha.

Yellow-frosted cupcakes are good for Cakes and Ale. If you bake your own, you can use brightly colored cupcake papers, and you can decorate the cakes themselves with sprinkles or create sunbursts on them with colored icing.

We like jalapeño cheese bread too (it has a slightly golden color and a hot taste). You can bake your own if it's not available commercially where you live. Just add cheddar cheese and jalapeño peppers to your favorite bread recipe. If you can't find jalapeño peppers, then any spicy pepper will do. Be careful if you are using hot-pepper flakes, though, as they tend to be hotter.

If you're looking for something more substantial, here's a recipe we modified from Dr. Andrew Weil's *Eating Well for Optimum Health*. Dr. Weil, for those readers who don't know, is the father of integrative medicine, which treats alternatives to Western medicine with respect, without scorning the clinical approach. His pioneering work at the University of Arizona has galvanized the movement, and now there are several clinics around the country whose doctors have been trained here in Tucson by Dr. Weil. This particular book illustrates his basic points about "eating well for optimum health" with what he calls healing stories, and he presents quite a few intriguing recipes! Canyondancer and I recommend *all* his books.

Summer Melon-Ball Soup

Dr. Weil's recipe is for "Summer Melon Soup." We've changed it a little bit, and we call it "Summer Melon-*Ball* Soup." We like it because it's a cold soup, because melons are sunny foods, and because it includes peppers (which we're inclined to put in nearly everything). To make it for Litha, you will need two ripe cantaloupes, cut in half and seeded. Remove the rind from only 2 halves of the cantaloupe, and dice them (it should give you about 4 cups). You will also need 4 cups of watermelon, seeded and diced (leave a portion of watermelon on the side, undiced); and two hot peppers, minced (or use up to 2 1/2 ounces of canned, diced green chilies). Finally, have about a 1/2 cup of raspberries (or blueberries or blackberries) on hand for a finishing touch to your soup.

To prepare the soup, begin by pureeing the diced cantaloupe and watermelon, and add a little lemon juice and honey to taste (you might even find it needs a dash of salt). Stir in the minced peppers, and chill the mixture in your refrigerator. Next, scoop the cantaloupe with the rinds and the uncut watermelon into balls. Serve your chilled soup with the melon balls, and add a few of the raspberries for garnish. Yum!

Symbols

Fire is one symbol for Litha. For the Druids, Fire is the Element that unites Earth, Air, and Water; for the Asatru, Fire was the more sacred because it was little known in the Northern lands. Fire represents heat, light, passion, growth, and life itself. It also represents civilization in that taming fire allowed humanity some measure of environmental control and the ability to develop domestic technologies such as cooking and metalworking. But let's look at more specific symbols.

Bonfires

Though it's not exclusive to mid-Summer, the bonfire is a more specific symbol of Litha than of the other Sabbats. Bonfires are traditionally used to celebrate Beltane and Samhain, too, and candles are particularly significant to Bride. Bonfires at Beltane represent not only the growing strength of the Sun, but also the burning passion of love that underlies the marriage of the Goddess and God. Samhain's bonfire is symbolically alchemical, symbolizing the transformation of death to gestation, as well as representing our faith that solar light and warmth will return to the world.

At Litha, bonfires symbolize the Sun and the peak of its strength. Building them is generally a community effort that involves more than the task of collecting and stacking the wood that will burn: You must also make sure that the bonfire is built where it can burn hugely without endangering homes, barns, public buildings, pastures, and the surrounding woods. There is also a fair amount of planning required for a successful bonfire—food must be prepared for the feast! Part of the mid-Summer abundance we celebrate includes the bountiful cooperation that the creation and enjoyment of a bonfire inspires. Part of the abundance of the Sun God's realm is everyone's contentment, and the bonfire symbolizes this as well as the strength of the God's solar aspect.

Flowers

In American culture, June is still the bridal month, and in some Traditions of Wicca, Litha, as well as Beltane, is a bridal Sabbat. Thus, flowers, primary among Beltane's symbols, are also symbols of Litha. Now, depending on where you live and what the climate is like, fresh flowers may be available for Sabbat altars from Ostara through Mabon. Yet, some newcomers to the Craft may find it confusing that flowers, along with some other articles and ideas, can symbolize more than one Sabbat. What about that?

Flowers make a good example of overlapping symbols, and through them we can explore the relationships between the Summer Sabbats in a little more depth. At Imbolc and Ostara there are early flowers, and they, along with still-closed buds, represent the Goddess's promise of rebirth remembered, the dawning hope of life renewed. Just like the bouquet of a wine yet unpoured suggests its full complexity, the buds and flowers of late Winter and early Spring symbolize reborn life's first hesitant breath.

At Beltane, the fuller blooms symbolize promise, newly flowering love, the fresh capacity for fertility and creativity of all sorts, and potential beginning to take shape. Not yet all fully unfolded, the flowers of Beltane are fragrant and delicate, and they still hold some surprises as to what their size, shape, and coloration will be. They will develop stronger nectars and more abundant pollen. We garland them with ribbons, for their stems are not fully leaved, and hopeful as May's flowers bid us be, the fields are far from full.

But at Litha, oh, our gardens overwhelm us with scent and color, with leaf, and, yes, even with thorn. Flowers are open wide now, embracing the light and the warmth of Summer, giving up their perfume and their rich hues to the rising heat. In climes where they are needful of extra water and shade to protect them from the too-strong Sun, they more than repay us for our care of them. Leaves are full-formed and vivid, and petals are broad and bright. Butterflies feast, and the bees immerse themselves and carry away the pollen that will feed their hives and bring the roses back again. The Earth is abundant, and Litha's flowers symbolize the joy and generosity of the Mother Goddess, the God's promise of consummation finally fulfilled.

Perhaps these seem like subtle differences, or maybe they seem obvious now you think about them. Of course, each flower has collected its own correspondences as our cultures have come to understand the natural world in a wider variety of ways, and that just deepens the symbolism at every Sabbat. This is as it should be—for by Winter, we'll be in the depths of meaning, far from Litha's bright focus on the sensual material world. In the meantime, incorporating all of Litha's symbols into our rites, we celebrate Summer heartily, as we do all the seasons of life.

Fresh Fruit

Tucson British Traditional Priest Rick Johnson teaches that fresh fruit is also a symbol of Litha. This makes sense: Most fruits are red, yellow, and orange, and they are either round like the Sun or elongated like another aspect of the Wiccan God. And who doesn't enjoy red watermelon, red and yellow apples, and bright oranges in the Summer—not to mention juices and lemonade.

Oak Trees

Many bonfires are made with oak wood, and the oak tree is another symbol of Litha; one of the God's aspects at mid-Summer is that of the Oak King. The oak tree has always been sacred to the Druids, who consider it to be the noblest of trees. (The bilé that stands in Druid Circles for the world tree is usually an oak staff. However, it may also be an ash staff. From the Celtic perspective, the ash represents a doorway to other realms. For the Asatru, the world tree is an ash.)

It's the oak, though, that represents Litha for Wiccans. It's in the oak that the sacred mistletoe grows. Mistletoe was most likely harvested at Samhain (see the introduction to Samhain in *Celebrating the Seasons of Life: Samhain to Ostara*). Its association with mid-Winter is probably due to its prolific growth in oak trees. It's the Oak King who surrenders the Year at Litha, though He reigns in our hearts and minds a little longer. Oak trees, in one form or another, grow nearly worldwide. My old *Webster's New World Dictionary* notes that in England (Wicca's "old country") the word *oak* is—or was—also slang for "door." As we all know, doors can be mundane or they can be magical.

The Sun Wheel

The Sun wheel, part of many Litha celebrations, is a delightful symbol for this season. Round like the Sun (and round like the mouths of cauldrons and chalices—symbols of the Goddess's womb), bright and burning like the hot, bright Sun, and rolling toward the West like the setting of the day and the setting of the Year, the Sun wheel also includes community in its symbolism. In some cultures, the wheel is made of cheese (yellow or white) to extend the symbolism of abundance.

The burning, rolling wheel is also symbolic of the changing of the seasons and of our merry celebration of this change. It's a way to share our blessings with each other, for the Sun wheel is generally arranged to pass by or before everyone present—its flames shining on all and its warmth reaching everybody. It's a way of bringing the life and strength of the Sun God into our midst. It symbolizes His immanence among us, reminding us that the Gods are a part of our mundane lives. It also represents planes and meanings beyond our physical experience.

(As a side note, there is a "dark side" to the Sun wheel: Its incarnation as a swastika. Since the Nazis appropriated it, this symbol has been linked to their horrifying philosophy and behavior. At one time, in various cultures, the swastika was a stylized symbol for the Sun. Now, because of the Nazis, it's a widely recognized sign of terror and evil. This is especially distressing to the Asatru, for whom the swastika was once a proud cultural symbol. Now, though, it tends to be a symbol for the Nazi-tru rather than the Asatru.)

Lammas

Lammas is given no special notice on secular calendars, but on the Wheel of the Year it's one of the cross-Quarter days, one of the four Greater Sabbats. It's also the beginning of Autumn (in Gaelic, *Samhain* means "end of Summer"). In the old days, when we recognized only two seasons (Samhain and Beltane), Beltane marked the beginning of Summer, and Samhain marked the beginning of Winter, or the *end of Summer*. On the modern Wiccan calendar, while Winter still begins at Samhain, Imbolc now marks Winter's end; while Summer still begins at Beltane, Lammas now marks Summer's end.

Most Wiccan Sabbats take their names from Gaelic languages. Yule and Litha are exceptions, and so is Lammas. *Lammas* is a contraction of the Anglo-Saxon words for "loaf mass," and refers to the honor paid to the first loaf of bread made from the grain of the year's harvest. If the God was wounded at Litha, He begins to die in earnest at Lammas. Some Traditions suggest that the God is "sacrificed" at Lammas, but this is a difficult concept for many Wiccans to reconcile with the promise of the *Charge* that "She asks naught of sacrifice."

Sacrifice means "to make sacred." When we hear the word, we tend to think of terrified victims on stone altars and a wild-eyed, knife-wielding Priest about to make the fatal thrust. We get this image from Hollywood, from the Old Testament, and from all kinds of stories in between. However, we also use the word less violently when referring to self-sacrificing volunteers and heroes, and this is closer to the sense in which Wiccans use the word when we describe the God's death as "sacrifice."

The idea is that the God dies willingly to His own rebirth, which incidentally makes it possible for all of us to live through another Winter. When we speak of the God's sacrifice in the hunt and the harvest, we're saying that His willingness to die makes His death sacred—makes it an offering—to life and rebirth. Our use of His death (at Lammas, our focus is on the bread we make of the harvested grain) is another aspect of the sacrifice, of making His death sacred.

Let's interrupt our discussion of Lammas here to talk a little bit about *sacrifice* in a broader sense. One of the problems I have, as a Wiccan Priestess, with this word is that although its root meaning is completely compatible with Wiccan thealogy, its popular meaning is incompatible.

And yet, there isn't really another word I can use if I don't want to offer a paragraph's explanation every time I use it. There's really no escaping the various biblical and B-movie images that have attached themselves to this word, and even when we use it in the mundane sense when referring to self-sacrifice, we're almost always talking about self-deprivation.

My thesaurus suggests other words for *sacrifice*. They include *offering*, *oblation*, and *homage*, and they also include *ritual slaughter* and *immolation*. Those first three are good (*homage*, in particular, is eminently suitable, but not generally understood to describe a religious experience). *Slaughter* and *immolation*, while occasionally being technically correct, really don't begin to convey the beauty of Wiccan ritual or the depth of its significance. For most people, these two words still conjure images of maniacal Priests and innocent victims. (Sigh.)

It seems to me that these understandings, especially the idea that we have to give up something we love, something we need, or something that will make our lives worse if we do not have it, harken back to the notion that we must suffer pain and grief in this life and in this world to achieve any lasting peace, glory, or joy in the next. This is not a premise of Wicca, and we don't often have (or take) the opportunity to make that clear when we're talking about our faith. Our "sacrifices" are really "sanctifications," and most of what we give to the Gods, we give as gifts to each other. Our "offerings" (I'm a little troubled by some of that word's associations too) are made from love, and not from any sense that we'd better make them "or else."

When the God dies, He's not sacrificing Himself for us in the way Christians understand Jesus to have died for them. There's no expiation involved here—no sins to be paid for. Sure, there's an exchange of energy, but this is the same exchange present each time you take a step or a breath. That's because the worlds are composed of various combinations of matter and energy; that's basic physics. It's not a bargain, and the premise isn't that we need saving. It's a relationship, and the premise is that we're all part of a wondrous, joyful, uplifting, gladsome cycle of life. The God's death is not bloody and painful; He walks no Via Dolorosa. It's actually more appropriate to liken the harvest to an orgasm, for in it there is both immediate satisfaction and the release of life-continuing seed.

Because Wicca holds the cycles of incarnate life holy, and because we believe that death is a growth mechanism that is part of the process of reincarnation, we don't think of the God's death as a tragedy. For that matter, we don't, in a thealogical sense, think of our own deaths as tragedies, or ends. We know that following every Winter will be another Spring, and the flowers that wilt as the seasons change will eventually bloom again. The God's sacrifice in the harvest is a gift—the gift of life to itself.

When we eat the bread made from the harvested grain (the grain that was alive with His spirit), we take His spirit into ourselves—literally, of course, but figuratively as well. "You are what you eat" is a retired catchphrase now, but in many ways it's still true. When we partake of Lammas bread, we are sharing in the God's "sacrifice," His act of "making sacred," in a number of ways. First, we're eating to stay alive, which is one way of giving His death meaning. Second, we are literally eating His seed—and in many old stories, eating the God-become-seed produces a magical pregnancy, from which results a rebirth of the God. Third, we are taking into ourselves His qualities and responsibilities to the world: We're making a type of "oral" contract to carry on His work of living in the service of life. In all these ways, our tasting of or feasting on the Lammas bread is a sacred act that helps us recognize the sacredness of life, death, and rebirth.

Although *Lammas* is an Anglo-Saxon name for this Sabbat, there is another name by which it is also known: the Celtic name *Lughnassadh*. (Spellings may vary slightly. It's pronounced either **Loona**-*saad* or *Loo*-**nass**-*aad*, according to personal and regional preferences. In both pronunciations, the final *d* is very close to silent.) This name for the Sabbat refers to games that, according to folklore, the Celtic Sun god Lugh established in honor of his mother.

These were games of speed and strength, such as races, tosses, and wrestling. We don't know exactly what the original motivation was, but we can imagine that as the Sun God's strength began to wane and He began to die in the harvest, a last show of strength was in order. We know that even in death—and proactively *through* death—the God, the cycle of life, sustains us, and sets an example of "sacrifice" to the community. The Lughnassadh games may then have been a demonstration of His lasting capacity to make these efforts. We can certainly interpret them this way now.

ore

As we have already established, the Celtic name for this particular Sabbat is *Lughnassadh*, relating it to a gathering in honor of the god Lugh. These assemblies were held all over Celtic Britain and Europe, and they functioned partly as the Northern "moots" and "things" did: as opportunities for disputes to be settled by tribal leaders. These gatherings were also fairs (just like in the song "Scarborough Fair" sung by Simon and Garfunkel), as well as occasions for lively games.

Games, similar to the ongoing Highland Games, are especially appropriate on this Sabbat, which is named after Lugh. One of his other names is Lugh Long-hand. He came to be called this name when he applied for a place in the royal court of the Tuatha de Danaan. Lugh suggested to them a variety of skills by which he might be qualified, but the court already had a smith, a carpenter, a bard, a healer, a champion, and a magician, as well as members who could do other things that Lugh was talented at doing. Lugh, however, was the only individual who was possessed of *all* those skills, and on that unique qualification, he was accepted into the pantheon.

Other stories tell us that he was called Lamhfhada—"long-armed"—because of his prowess with a magical spear, making him an outstanding warrior. One of his significant victories was the defeat of his own grandfather, the Fomorian king who was first a conqueror of Ireland, and then an oppressor. Despotic kings in the days of lore often heard the prophecy that they'd be overcome by a grandson, and their standard reaction was to isolate their daughters. (If their daughters didn't have children, there would be no grandsons; therefore, they would not run the risk of being overthrown.) It always backfired, though, and so it did for King Balor: His daughter Eithne came to be Lamhfhadsa's mother. In some versions of the tale, Lamhfhadsa kills Balor by putting out his poison eye (so large it took four men to lift its lid and allow its deadly gaze to fall on enemies) with a slingshot. In other versions, he accomplishes the deed with his magical spear, with which he is still depicted to this day. (Some scholars and Traditions believe that with a spear as an "attribute," Lugh may have had a thunder-god aspect too. Then again, one who is the master of so many useful skills might be "thunderous" in his capacity to meet a community's needs.)

Another interesting, if superficial and speculative, correspondence is that of Lud, one of Lugh's English names. While this may refer to his thunder-god aspect, it's fascinating to me that Lud is the craftsman's craftsman, and that, in the 18th and 19th centuries, those who resisted the Industrial Revolution's beginnings in the textile business because they feared diminished wages and unemployment were called Luddites. While the movement was most likely named after Ned Ludd, the individual who first destroyed a couple of mechanized weaving frames, it is very likely that Ned's family name was old and may have carried with it the sentiment, if not the fact or even the conscious memory, of the god Lud's jack-of-all-trades nature.

It's told that Lugh established the August games—funeral games—in honor of his mother. The lady in question is not his bio-magical mother, but his foster mother, Tailtiu. In her role as a foster mother, she might be a secularized Mother Goddess, and the establishment of the games, which could be described as an explosion of male energy, may be a desexed reference to the Sun God's fertilization of the fields. We may never fully understand the metaphorical contortions required of chroniclers who wanted to preserve earlier cultures without offending medieval monotheism. But modern Pagans can and do "retro-interpret" the old tales and see references in them to the natural relationships among the seasons, the forces of life, the universe, and everything.

Kirk Thomas, liturgist for Tucson's Sonoran Sunrise Grove of ADF Druids, refers us to another story about Lammas: "This is the time," he says, "that the King would 'marry' the Goddess of Sovereignty. In Ireland, the new King would mate with a mare. Then the mare would be killed and made into broth. The King would sit in the broth and give it, with his hands, to his people."

Our first reaction to this story might be, "Well, yuck." But when you think about it, the mare represents the Goddess. (See the section about Litha's lore for more about horses.) The king's mating with the mare represents a marriage to the land, which conveyed the king's authority.

Whether this mating was a literal act or a symbolic act is not known for sure. I, for one, choose to believe it was symbolic, if only because the logistics would deprive the literal act of any kingly dignity at all. Killing the mare—a sacred animal—and partaking of the broth parallels harvesting the crops and eating the bread made from them. Sharing this wealth with his people was the king's duty. To prove himself worthy of his life among the literal and figurative riches of his realm, he needed to dispense their blessings among the people. Symbolically, this is not unlike the Native American potlatch, where the chief gives away his riches to the tribe, and, in so doing, demonstrates his natural authority and fitness to rule.

The Druids in Tucson have a magnificent stead at which to symbolically reenact kingship rites, but not every Neo-Pagan has such resources; and not every Neo-Pagan relies upon any of the Celtic myths. Many Asatru, for instance, have taken to holding their Freysfest on July 31. This is a *blot*, or festival, for Freyr (sometimes called Frey), which of old was not tied to a particular part of the year.

It's appropriate to celebrate a festival for Freyr at Lammas-tide because Freyr is a fertility god, the brother of the fertility and Moon goddess Freya. Also, there are parallels to some of our Celtic myths in Freyr's story. First, his wife, Gerda, was a daughter of a giant whose clan Freyr had to battle in order to win her. Second, Freyr's chariot was drawn by two boars. Finally, reminiscent of Lugh's many skills and talents, and of Manawyddan's craftsmanship, Freyr is said to have possessed a boat that not only could hold all the gods, but which could also be folded up!

At harvest time, corn and grain is often gathered in *stooks*, or teepee-shaped bundles. Other crops are sometimes piled in mounds. These mounds can look like burial mounds, and so they are in a certain sense because they represent the death of the crops that are harvested. But in the Wiccan understanding of the world, a grave is a womb, for the Earth is the body of the Goddess. From Her, we—and our God—are reborn. Seeds and roots beget their own rebirth, from the Earth, to the Earth.

Mounds are also entries to and, in some cases, the palaces of the Otherworld, the Land of Youth, where the immortal gods and fairies live. At Lammas, we celebrate the beginning of the harvest season: The first grains and fruits are gathered and enjoyed, and the chill of Winter, directing us to introspection, is not yet upon us. Lammas-tide is a mystical confluence of the fading Summer and the impending Winter. Though harvest has begun, there's yet time to play. But the play is in earnest, for the reaping of both game and field does matter. Indeed, the games and feasts of Lammas are often conducted at or nearby to mounds, such as the Mound of Tailtiu in Ireland.

The sacrificial king is one of the themes of Lammas. In the days of lore, a king could not rule without the Goddess's authority, which we know was conveyed through a sacred marriage. The king could also not rule if he suffered any imperfection. From even older days came the idea that a successful king's reign should be ended before it failed (quit while you're ahead, we still hear today), and that his very essence, his flesh and blood, should be used to ensure the fertility of the land. This is something to think about the next time you fertilize your yard!

In Celtic legends, Lugh and his counterparts were wounded before they were killed. Permit me another slight digression here to note and briefly explore the idea that gods—immortals—don't die naturally, but they could be, and often were, killed or "transformed." This is a confusing idea to a lot of people: If gods are gods, how can they die? Well, the notion that a god *can* die is actually a universal theme, if you think about it. We have enough stories of gods who die and are resurrected to realize this. The Wiccan God is all that dies and is reborn. He is divine, magical, and sacred precisely because He dies and is reborn. He is, like we are, immortal through His cycle, not because He is incapable of dying.

Complementing His mortality, the Goddess experiences death by Her participation in His seasons. Her immortal transformations show us the eternal face of life and death, shows us that death is but the new phase of the Moon. So when we wonder how it is that gods can die, we're asking the wrong question. What we should be scratching our heads about is how we think we can die without being reborn, for every hint our God and Goddess gives us makes it clear that we will be born again.

The harvest itself is symbolic of the Grain God's death, and death's clear promise of rebirth. It is with this symbolism that many Wiccans celebrate Lammas and the beginning of the harvest season.

ituals

A Harvest Rite With Your Coven

One of our Lammas activities is to create a field of wheat and a scythe from construction paper and other easy-to-find materials. The following ritual uses those crafts. You'll need the usual accoutrements of a Circle for this rite, along with your wheat field and your scythe. Set your altar at North to leave plenty of room in the center of your Circle. If you'd like to be just a little eccentric, set your altar at Southwest (this is unconventional, but it is appropriate for a Lammas rite).

You will also need some corn bread and fresh strawberries for Cakes, along with an appropriate Ale to share. If you have a cauldron, place it at Southwest, and hide your Cakes (corn bread and strawberries) and Ale in it. (This rite can be performed indoors, although depending on your options for furniture re/arrangement, you may have to work a little harder to accommodate a smaller space.)

Cast your Circle as you usually do (you may choose to follow the guidelines in Appendix A of *Celebrating the Seasons of Life: Samhain to Ostara*, or Appendix A of this volume). Whether you set up the field of wheat before you come to the Circle or as part of the work once the Circle is cast, however formally or informally, is up to you. In any case, your accordion-folded rows of paper wheat should fill the center of the Circle, leaving enough room to walk around the "field" and between the rows. Each row will likely consist of at least two, and probably more, sheets of construction paper wheat so that there will be some wheat for everyone present to harvest. If you're celebrating as a solitary, you'll be able to appreciate the burdens of smaller farms, on which each individual has a lot of work to do!

Before you acknowledge that we've come to the beginning of the harvest season, you'll want to reinforce the impression that the rows of folded construction paper before you are, in fact, fields ready to cut.

Begin by holding the bowl of salt at North, sprinkle some across the field, and say, "This field was plowed and planted with seed." (The salt represents both earth and seed.)

Holding the bowl of water at East, make a windy, whooshing sound, use your fingers to spritz a few drops onto the field, and say, "By rains blown upon the wind, this field was watered in its need."

Holding a candle aloft at South, say, "By sunlight through the Summer, this crop was warmed upon the plain."

Standing at West and spreading your arms wide to show off the ripe field, say, "Now this cooperation has yielded a mighty crop of grain!"

Everyone present can then ooh and ahh in appreciation of the mighty crop. If your group is at all theatrically inclined, someone might want to remark about the backbreaking work of weeding and organic pest control.

You can then declare Lammas, and the harvest season it opens, like this (or use words of your own, remembering that words from your heart are always more powerful than words from anybody's book):

> Harvest Sabbat, first of three, first of fruit, and first of grain;
> We the reapers and trustees, transfiguring the God's domain.
> We hail the Lammas, loaf and fruit!
> The Green God's death for life salute!

Whether everyone present has their own scythe or the group is sharing one, it will be up to the Priestess to decide who gets to "cut" the first "stalks of wheat." While waiting their turns, everyone else can shoulder their scythes so no one accidentally pokes someone else and so no "blades" are accidentally broken. Everyone can chant while each person takes a turn (a solitary should chant as he or she reaps). A chant many Wiccans already know, "Horned One, Lover, Son, Leaper in the Corn, deep in the Mother, die and be reborn," is certainly appropriate now.

You might also make up your own chant, or use this one, to any of several easy tunes you like:

> He falls to the blade and is remade
> in seed and flour and bread;
> no need for grief, He's reborn from the sheaf!
> By His life our lives are fed.

As each row of grain is cut, the reaper gathers (folds) it and sets it as upright as possible in the cauldron. (It's especially nice when the tops of the stalks of wheat show above the rim of the cauldron.) Depositing the harvest into the cauldron not only simulates taking sheaves of wheat to a barn or threshing floor, but also the God's death and return to the womb of the Mother. (In some Traditions of Wicca, the God dies and is mourned at Lammas; in others, He is not considered dead until Mabon, which occurs during the hunting season, so that He dies at that time in His animal forms as well as His vegetable aspects.)

When the wheat has been harvested, the Priest, facing the center of the Circle, holds his hands over the cauldron containing the harvested grain, and says:

> *Grain to kernel, wheat to flour;*
> *life from death at harvest's hour.*
> *Red the fruit and gold the meal:*
> *Rebirth begins in commonweal.*
> *Hail the wine! And hail the Cake!*
> *Hail the life we cannot take!*

As he finishes this incantation, the Priest brings forth from the cauldron into which the harvested grain has gone, or from behind it if the cauldron is too small, a plate of corn bread and strawberries, and a glass of "wine" or "ale." To the cheers and huzzahs of all present, the Priestess takes the Cakes and Ale to the altar, where she and the Priest proceed to consecrate and share them in the coven's usual way.

Lammas Alone

Harvest is traditionally a community activity, so it might seem difficult to celebrate a harvest Sabbat on your own. However, it is acceptable to practice Wicca solitary: It is our understanding that none of us is ever really alone, even if there's no one else in the room with us. Here's one way to celebrate Lammas when you're the only one in your Circle.

For this ritual you'll need your usual altar gear and an orange. (If you'd rather, you can use an apple. If you do use an apple, core it and slice it into eight sections ahead of time, and then assemble the pieces to look like it's whole again. Bring it into the Circle this way so you can pretend it's segmenting during the rite, just as an orange would.) The fruit is not for Cakes and Ale, so remember to have your usual provisions for that portion of the rite.

After you've invoked the Goddess and God, declare the Sabbat something like this:

At Lammas-tide, I start to reap
that which I sowed at Sabbats past.
Some I'll share and some I'll keep
of what I months ago broadcast.
I celebrate first harvest's feast
and count my blessings one by one:
from the greatest to the least,
it's now the harvest has begun.

Not for weeks will Winter come;
in the fields some crops still grow;
At Lammas, gently comes Autumn,
and in the Sun's light we still glow.
Some things are ripe; some yet increase.
I use what's full, await the rest.
There's nourishment in all of these,
and by them all my life is blessed.
This fruit before me represents
the measure of the year gone by.
As I eat, I'll be content,
and harvest trust to satisfy.

Now take a moment to think back over the last 12 months. How did last year's harvest keep you through the Winter? What plans did you make during those Winter months when the focus was inward? What did you plant in your life last Spring? What effort did you give to the nurture of your crops? Do the fruits of your labor satisfy you now? Does it look like your efforts paid off, and does it look as though you'll be comfortable during the coming Winter?

Do you have doubts? Remember that Lammas is the first harvest, and there's still time to gather more from your fields, whether you are thinking about a real garden or your social, financial, or emotional growth or gleanings. If things have gone wrong, there's still time to figure out why, and maybe you can salvage something positive from mistakes or disaster.

Consider first what plans you had for the harvest you're gathering now. As you eat the first segment of your orange, remember your intent to find a better job, finish that remodeling project, open yourself to new relationships, or whatever goal you were striving for. Remember and acknowledge that intention, and appreciate its worth as you savor the first piece of fruit.

As you eat the second piece, think about the visions you have of success in these projects. Remember the thought of a grand corner office, the comments you imagined hearing from your friends when they saw the work you'd done on your house, or how you dreamed of sitting under the stars with a new love or enjoying a movie with a new friend.

Eating the next few pieces, think back on what you did to realize your goals. If your fingertips turned black with ink from looking at so many classified ads in the paper, chuckle at the recollection. If you took a class at a building supply store so you'd know how to tackle that remodeling project, remember the concentration you shared with other do-it-yourselfers. If you found volunteer work, joined a book club, or signed up for a class and met people who share your interests, think about how much fun it's been talking to them.

Even if you haven't found a new job yet, even if there's more remodeling work to do, and even if you haven't found a partner or you're still working to revitalize a relationship too important to give up on, every effort you made toward your goal is part of your harvest, and this is something to celebrate. Every step you took was an offering of good faith. Every experience you had has taught you something (learning is noble and wisdom is worth a lot when it's dark and cold outside *or* inside). Those projects underway count for something in your assessment and appreciation of your harvest!

As you eat another segment of fruit, taste the sweetness of goals fully accomplished. Congratulate yourself on the new job, on the job completed, or on the completion you feel with a partner. Maybe, as you came closer to realizing them, your goals changed. If this happened, congratulate yourself on recognizing it and on learning more about what you really want. That's an excellent aspect of harvest.

As you finish the next-to-last segment of your orange, savor the pulp and the juice, and appreciate the ways your life has changed, even if they weren't the changes you expected to make. The best-laid plans of mice and men "gang oft aglee," as Robert Burns says in his poem "To a Mouse." In other words, they "go oft awry," or, basically, "stuff happens." Some "stuff" that happens is beyond our control. If we're talking about literal fields of wheat, "stuff" includes drought, flood, and gale-force winds, not to mention insects, rodents, and blight. If we're talking about metaphorical "crops," a lot more things can go wrong without it being our own fault. Indeed, what counts then—what will keep us going during fallow and barren times—is knowing that we did the best we could under the circumstances. So if you've been coping with unexpected change or your plans have gone "aglee," remember that you have harvested self-control, creativity, and grace under pressure, and that you definitely have something to celebrate!

At this point you should have one segment of orange left. Pause again. Ask yourself whether things have gone brilliantly for you. Has everything worked out just the way you wanted it to, details and all? Or, have things worked out close enough to what you hoped for? Well, either way that's fabulous! Hard work and merit always count, even if they don't always get us what we work for or deserve. Share whatever you have with your friends and community, whether it is material comfort or boundless optimism, and you'll find your harvest is a successful one.

Think about the ways you can share your harvest. Can you give advice from experience? Can you pay for dinner? Can you teach somebody how to do something they need to do? Can you support a friend just by listening? Don't eat the last segment of your orange until you can think of two or three ways to share your harvest! When you have realized the number of ways you can share yourself with others, notice how the last segment of orange you eat tastes just a bit better than all the others.

When your orange is gone, recite the following (remember that using your own words is always at least a little better than even the best words other people give you as examples):

> *Hail to Lammas; harvest, hail!*
> *Blessed be the first-picked fruit!*
> *Blessed be the hard travail,*
> *and blessed be the living root.*
> *Bless the furrow, bless the blade;*
> *bless the God, for He must wane.*
> *Bless the table all a-lade,*
> *and bless the Wheel that turns again!*

Now it's time to conduct the rite-within-a-rite of Cakes and Ale as you normally would. Finally, dismiss the Quarters, thank the Gods, and close your Circle.

Lammas With Non-Pagans

If you're including non-Pagans in a much more subtle and informal ritual, you won't need an altar per se, but you will need to have a bowl of water, some salt (or cornmeal), and a candle on hand. You will also need strawberries and corn bread to eat, and a "field of wheat" and "scythe" made of construction paper (directions for making these two crafts may be found in the section with activities for Lammas). Instead of casting a Circle, simply walk the circumference of a circle that defines the boundaries of your "field," noting the Directions as you pass them so that everyone present is compass-oriented.

The same way as described in the directions for celebrating a harvest rite with your coven, someone at North should sprinkle a bit of salt (or cornmeal) on the ground and say, "Planting the field!" Then one or more people can set up the rows of wheat made of construction paper. Next, someone standing at East should sprinkle the wheat with water and say, "It needs rain to grow!" Someone else can hold a candle at South and say, "Without sunshine, no yield!" And again, at West, someone else can show wide-armed appreciation of the grain's growth, saying, "A full crop to show!"

Now it's time to harvest the ripened grain in your field. Again, you may share a scythe, or each person celebrating may have their own. Encourage any children who are participating to work gently, rather than hacking about as they see characters do in many cartoons and video games. You might like to introduce this part of the "ritual" by saying something like this:

> *Now it's time to cut the corn*
> *that will become the bread we eat.*
> *Next Spring we'll plant another field*
> *from seed we'll save from this year's wheat!*

In the same way as you would in an openly Wiccan ritual, ask the harvesters to fold their wheat and tuck it into a cauldron (or a cooking pot). This cauldron should be placed within the boundaries of your field.

If it is large enough, place the strawberries and corn bread inside it. If the cauldron is too small, keep the fruit and bread close by it.

Instead of the "miracle rhyme" you'd use in a religious Lammas rite, say this when you're ready to acknowledge the transformation:

> *The grain to harvest's cutting falls*
> *to make the bread for banquet halls.*
> *We'll save some seeds where life's waiting,*
> *and plant a new field come next Spring.*
> *We shared the work we needed to do,*
> *and now we'll share the eating too!*

Before you actually eat the strawberries and corn bread, someone, or everyone, should say:

> *Thank you, fruit, and thank you, bread—*
> *for making sure that we are fed!*

Of course, if any of the people in your non-Pagan group are aggressively Christian, they may feel a need to rephrase this blessing to specifically mention their God. That's alright—we *do* all have to work together to make this world a comfortable place for everyone. Plus, we can never really give *too much* thanks for enough to eat and friends to eat it with.

Lammas Vow

Lammas marks the beginning of Autumn, and no matter how subtly, the death of harvest begins to overtake Summer's vitality. Animals that will be hibernating through the Winter are starting to gorge and to store away provisions, and migrations are beginning. Lammas is the first of Wicca's three harvest festivals: Some crops are coming ripe already.

Fields begin to turn from green to gold, while flowers go to seed and fall to the ground. The hours of daylight are shortening noticeably now. The Goddess, in some myth cycles, begins to grieve in anticipation of the God's impending death (and yet there are still glorious days that seem to make time stand still). Her joy in His life is still evident in the last of Summer's blooms and wines, yet She witnesses the inevitability of Winter as well.

Not yet do we see the apparent barrenness of Winter, or even the brilliance of leaves' red and gold mourning. But, looking around, we realize that before there can be rebirth in the Spring (Imbolc is across the Wheel from Lammas), there must be the dying, and the rest that follows it. Remember that the name of this Sabbat, *Lammas*, is from the Anglo-Saxon words for "loaf mass," and this mass is in celebration of a loaf made from life we know is waning.

We have shared our energies with the world all Summer and spurred various efforts toward growth. Now we need to see what Summer projects are still unfinished and whether we might still be able to complete them this season. It's time to begin gathering our energies to ourselves again. During these last warm days, we should rejoice in what we have produced from our Summer activities. Yes, there's a chill in the air at night now, and we know we need to think about how we'll stay warm in the coming months. Yet, there's still a little time for growth as we start to orient ourselves toward the harvest, and we can—we ought to, we must—take pleasure in the work we've done to supply our hearts and minds (as well as our bodies) for the Winter.

A cautionary tale often told at this time of year, I've never liked Aesop's fable about the Ant and the Grasshopper for two reasons. First, at least in some versions, the Ant seems so terribly self-righteous and sure of his superiority while being so callous about the Grasshopper's fate. Second, in most versions, the tale diminishes the value of joy, of fun, and of recreation. The *Charge of the Goddess* speaks of "mirth *and* reverence." Surely it's a balance we should be aiming for—certainly it's balance that the Wheel carries us to next. At Lammas, we can anticipate the Sun's farewell, but it's wrong, I think, to be heedless of our essential longing to harvest rapture along with the rye.

Take the Lammas Vow as you gather the first harvest from your garden, or as you enjoy home-baked bread privately with your family, or in Circle. It's always appropriate (but more so at Lammas) to celebrate with Cakes you've blended and baked yourself and with Ale you've brewed at home, too, if that's possible. If you can't bake your own bread, make the following vow as an offering you seal by partaking of something fresh from a local bakery:

The Wheel rolls more, and Autumn returns.
Cooler the rain; the Sun lower burns.
The coloring leaves presage the Year:
all things move into harvest's sphere.
I vow to savor fruits first picked;
nor into grief shall I be tricked.
I vow to offer what once I spurred,
and face the Turning reassured.

ctivities

On the Wheel of the Year, Lammas (the first harvest celebration) marks the beginning of Autumn, the start of the harvest season. Thus, it makes sense to celebrate Lammas with an enactment of harvest.

If you have your own crops—whether they are in a field, a small garden plot, or in a pot on a balcony or windowsill—by all means hold your ritual among them. Let your literal mini-harvest represent the larger work that farm communities of old would have done around the first of August. You will be able to adapt at least one of the rituals in the preceding section to fit a field site. Most of us, though, even if we can celebrate outside on a deck, a patio, or in a backyard, don't have ripe fields of grain to work with. Therefore, we need to craft our own fields. Here is one way of doing it:

Paper Wheat

You'll need large 11 × 18-inch sheets of construction paper in tan, yellow, beige, or orange colors. You'll also need scissors, a pencil with an eraser, crayons or colored markers, the cardboard tube from the center of a roll of wrapping paper, and a piece of cardboard such as you might find on the back of a writing tablet.

Begin by cutting several sheets of the construction paper in half, lengthwise. Put the pieces together in pairs, one atop of the other. (You can even stack three or four together if you think you will be able to cut easily through them.) Now, along one edge, sketch a "wheat design" with your pencil. Once you have it sketched to your satisfaction, cut it out, and then make wide accordion folds in the wheat-edged strips so they'll stand up on the floor. Cut five or six unattached, whole stalks of wheat (with stems) to bundle later. When you stand the folded pages of wheat in your Circle, you'll lean the full stalks against the folds so they seem to be standing up with the rest.

Mind you, this takes some careful cutting, but even so, it's not as much work as actually plowing, sowing, tending, and harvesting a crop of wheat or other grains. (You could also devise easier ways to create your own wheat field. The thought you put into it will count as an offering, too, even though you are aiming to make the project less labor-intensive.) As an alternative, you may create a field of corn instead of a field of wheat. Wiccan chants for the harvest season do refer to "corn and grain," but in Wicca's old countries, "corn" was what we now call "wheat," so harvesting either or both is appropriate.

Because cutting several rows of corn or grain out of construction paper is a tedious task, if you can't share it with other members of your coven or family, it's best to allow a few days to get it done so your cutting hand doesn't cramp! Use crayons or markers to add the details of individual kernels and to color to the leaves. If you're making a field of corn, you might even like to add a few strands of yarn or embroidery thread to simulate the corn silk! How elaborately you do this is up to you. You can also find pictures of wheat or corn in clip art or old magazines, cut them out, paste them onto your construction paper, and then cut the construction paper to follow a rough outline of the picture. It's alright if this project takes some time and energy, but it shouldn't turn into an odious chore, nor should the pressure of doing it "just so" discourage you from doing it at all.

Next, you will make a scythe with which to harvest your corn and grain. On the piece of cardboard, draw half a crescent—from the pointy end to the middle, positioning the widest part of the half-crescent on an edge of the cardboard—and cut it out. This will be the blade of your scythe. Cut a slot into one end of the cardboard tube from the wrapping paper, and slide the wide end of your "blade" into it. If you'd like, cover the exposed part of the scythe blade with tinfoil to simulate metal. (It's true that real scythe blades aren't made of bright, silvery metal, but this harvest is theatrically symbolic, and so is your scythe.)

Harvest Photo Album or Scrapbook

For this project, you can make your own photo album from black construction paper. You can also buy a ready-made photo album or a scrapbook kit, which you can find in most craft stores. If you're buying a picture album, though, make sure it's "archival," or it will eventually turn your photos green or allow them to fade beyond recognition.

If you choose to create a photo album, try pairing photos together that show how much a child has grown since the beginning of the calendar year, since last Samhain, or since last Lammas. If you're one of those families who still marks children's growth with pencil marks on doorjambs, take a photo of each child pointing to his or her earlier and present marks. You could also take a picture of each child holding up the clothes they have outgrown. If a youngster in your family has recently attended a first dance, that "prom picture" deserves a place in this album. Photos from camp, family vacations, and birthday parties also belong here. If you have lost weight on a diet, include "before and after" photos. Same goes if you have cut your long hair or if you have let your short hair grow out.

What are you reaping this year, and what are the first signs of your harvest? Did you learn to cook a few basic dishes? Good for you! Now set the table and have someone photograph you while you are cooking, or simply take a photo of your pots on the stove with their lids on if you can't prepare the food when you're taking the picture. Or the next time you serve your family or guests, ask them to hold up their forks and smile while you take a photo. Maybe your spouse or an older child can take a picture of you in the kitchen, either busy at the stove or measuring ingredients. Don't forget you can take more than one picture or keep more than one memento to illustrate your harvest!

Is your accomplishment intangible? If you think about it, you will eventually come up with an appropriate way to illustrate it. Maybe you've come through some hard times, with nothing much to show for it but a better mood? Pose for a picture in which you look sad, and then another in which you look happy. Put these photographs side by side in your album. You can cut an arrow out of construction paper to point from one photo to the other, or add a colorful exclamation mark to emphasize the happy picture. You can also add captions, cut from magazines, that capture the mood of your photo or describe your harvest to a T. Or use those wonderful gel pens that show up so well on dark paper to explain your photos and other souvenirs in your own handwriting.

When creating a scrapbook, include photos, personal poems, "scraps" collected from your travels, etc. Include originals or photocopies of items such as college acceptance letters or good recommendations from former bosses or coworkers (these are viewable mementos of long-awaited, hard-worked-for events and accomplishments). The best scrapbooks, I think, hold more than just photos!

Remember, your scrapbook, just like a photo album, doesn't have to be about a "harvest" that other people can recognize. Maybe you've been doing a lot of "inner work," and its meaning and significance is better expressed in visual symbols—your own photos or scenic pictures from magazines—than in, say, a diary that depends on words. For the last half-century at least, as people have moved away from farms, most of us have been celebrating more personal and symbolic harvests than we have been gathering in harvests of grains, fruits, and vegetables. And although we do find comfort and encouragement in sharing the progress of our personal harvests with our families, covens, and friends, the point of remembering them in scrapbooks is to comfort and encourage ourselves. Like parents who need an occasional visitor to remind them how much their children have changed since the last time they visited, sometimes we need to be reminded how much we've grown too. Keeping a harvest scrapbook helps!

Scrapbooking helps you keep track of and take stock of your life. That's why, though I keep scrapbooks year-round, I've included it as a harvest activity. The connection is that Lammas is the first harvest festival on Wicca's Wheel of the Year (two more harvest festivals follow, and, in my mind, that makes Lammas a good time to take stock).

Is there a part of your life under-represented in your photo album or scrapbook? Make an effort to get pictures or save some "scraps" to honor all the things you do! Are there photos you'd like to see included, but they haven't been taken 'cause you haven't been to that place or done that activity yet? Go there, do that—or start getting ready to! As the photos and the harvest begin to come in, we can get an idea of how well-provisioned we'll be for the Winter, and if there's a need yet unfulfilled, there's still time to add to what we have to gather!

Lammas Leis

In the middle of writing this book, I learned a craft that seems to me well-suited for Lammas. I learned it from "Rose the Craft Lady" on a Hawaiian cruise that Canyondancer and I took in February of 2004. I'll explain how to make a woven lei, but first I want to tell you what Rose told us about the leis she showed us how to create. In Hawaiian tradition, she said, the first lei you make, of any kind, is yours to keep, but the ones you make after that are to be given away. I hope that Rose would agree that sharing the way to weave this lei is a way of "giving away."

When you're done weaving your lei, you'll notice little *X*s in its pattern, and I hope you relate those little *X*s to the Rune Gifu (also known as Gebo), which you'll read about later in the section about Mabon activities.

For this craft, you will need 2 pieces of grosgrain ribbon, each 3/8-inch wide and a little over 4 1/2 yards in length. Each piece can be the same color, two different colors, patterned ribbon, or any combination of solid and patterned. The only other supplies you'll need are a yardstick and a pair of scissors to measure and cut the lengths of ribbon.

Take your first piece of ribbon and start by measuring a little more than the length of your hand "in" from one end. At that spot, tie the ribbon into a loose knot, and set it aside. On the second ribbon, measure "in" from the end about the same distance, and make a loop about 2 inches long. Next, slide the nearly-tied knot you made in the first ribbon over the loop on the second ribbon, and tighten the knot. (See illustration.) *Please Note*: In the photographs for this craft, for clarity, Ribbon One is a lighter color and Ribbon Two is darker.

What you should be looking at now is a loop at the end of one ribbon, like a stick-figure head, tied at the "neck" with one end of the second ribbon. The remaining short ends of both ribbons should be approximately the same length, and so will the remaining long ends. You are going to be working with the long

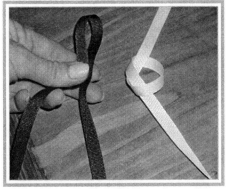

To begin, tie a knot in Ribbon One and form a loop in Ribbon Two.

ends, so you can ignore the short ends—but don't let them interfere when you are working with the longer ends!

Now, hold the loop—which is on Ribbon Two—in one hand, and take the long end of the other ribbon—Ribbon One—and poke it through the loop to make another loop. Switch hands, and take the long end of Ribbon Two, and poke it through the loop you just made with Ribbon One.

Then pull the end of Ribbon One tight, and you'll see that it forms what looks like a little square. (This project sounds more difficult than it really is, so be patient with yourself, and refer to the photographs!)

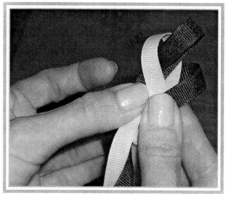

The knot is tied around the loop in Ribbon Two, and you should have tucked a loop of Ribbon One through a loop in Ribbon Two and tightened it. Now, make another loop with Ribbon Two, and put it through the new (and still empty) loop of Ribbon One.

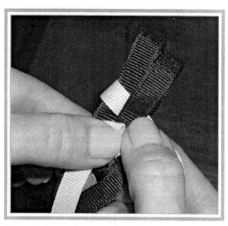

Now tighten the very first loop you made (the one you tied off with a knot). If you don't see a pattern forming yet, start again. It may take some practice to keep the ribbons straight and to get the hang of it.

Next, tighten the very first loop you made (the one in Ribbon Two that is tied off by Ribbon One). That knot will have loosened a bit by now: Don't untie it, but do pull on the short end of Ribbon Two to tighten that loop. At the other end, you still have a loop in Ribbon Two. Make a loop with the long end of Ribbon One, slip it through this loop in Ribbon Two, and then pull the long end of Ribbon Two. This will tighten the loop in Ribbon Two around the stem of the loop you just made in Ribbon One, and it will leave you with a loop in Ribbon One. (See illustration.)

There is a pattern here that I hope you can see by now. You are making a loop with one ribbon, and then slipping it through the existing loop in the other ribbon. Then, when you pull gently on the long end of the loop you have just slipped another loop through, you use that same long end to make the next loop, which will then slip through the untightened one. (See illustration.)

Don't be too frustrated if it takes you a few tries to get the hang of it. When I learned this craft on the cruise ship, the assembled class had the advantage of someone actually demonstrating and helping us one-on-one, and it still took some of the participants a long time to catch on. If you are patient with yourself (and these instructions), you will see how it works. Once you get the hang of it, you'll find that this is very, very easy. It's a lot of fun too, and after reading about it as a Lammas activity, I'm sure you'll find that it is easy to adapt this craft to be appropriate for any of Wicca's Sabbats.

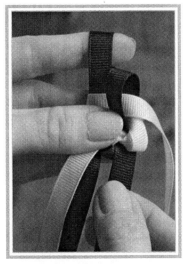

At Lammas, whether your ribbons are different colors or the same, you can let one of them represent the aspects of harvest that have come to fruition, and let the other symbolize those elements that still need a little work. One ribbon could represent the security of your relationship, *You are making a loop with one ribbon, and then slipping it through the loop in the other ribbon, which you then tighten.*

your job, or your Neo-Pagan path, and the other could stand for the reliable transportation, the better job, or the advanced education you still need to weave into your life.

One ribbon could symbolize your material accomplishments, such as projects you've completed, good grades you worked hard for, a new job or a promotion you earned, or better living conditions. The other ribbon could represent less tangible accomplishments, such as a new direction taken, a relationship improved, or an emotional issue resolved. Perhaps you'll let the two ribbons stand for two seemingly conflicting aspects of your life, and as you weave the ribbons together, you'll begin to harvest an understanding of the way those aspects of your life can be complements rather than opposites.

To finish the lei, instead of continuing to slip one loop through another, pull the ribbon all the way through the last loop—you'll want about as much ribbon left at the end as you had left over on your short ends at the beginning. Tie the matching short ends together—each color to its match, if you're using two colors—so that the lei stays flat. Once the knots are secure, you can trim them as closely as you like. (See the following illustrations.)

There's an aspect of harvest—which is, remember, as much a process as it is an event—that isn't often given much consideration, but is well-demonstrated by this craft, and that's the combining of separate elements to make a new whole. This project intertwines two ribbons to make a single lei, and part of the work of harvest is to combine various products of harvest to make new items: Flour (which is made of wheat) combines with butter (which is made from milk harvested from cows) and eggs (harvested from chickens) to make bread. This is the literal foundation of Lammas. But figuratively and symbolically in this ribbon lei, we can let it remind us that harvest is more than gathering ripe fruits and veggies.

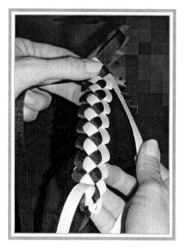

Here is a partially completed lei, in which you can see the pattern.

To finish your lei, pull the end of one ribbon all the way through the last loop, making sure not to make a new one. Tie the matching short ends together so the lei doesn't twist.

Our lives go through a process of growth and harvest, and it's not enough to simply "cut the wheat." We have to do more than move into a great apartment or house; we have to make it a home. We have to do more than find a better job; we have to make it part of our lives and put something of ourselves into it. We have to do more than fall in love; we have to work on the relationship. Ingredients are worth much more when we combine them, not only with each other, but with our own effort, to make something of them. Harvest is partly about the whole being greater than the sum of its parts.

This craft shows us this quite plainly. No one's impressed by two lengths of ribbon, no matter how pretty the colors. But you're sure to get at least one or two comments of "Oh, cool! How'd you do that?" when you show off your lei. Put the same effort into your harvest and making something of it, and you'll feel the same way about your life too.

Lammas Recipes

On the four-season Wiccan calendar, Lammas marks the beginning of Autumn. It's the cross-Quarter day between Litha, the Summer Solstice, and Mabon, the Autumn Equinox. It's a day of transition, and our feast recipes can reflect this.

Blueberry Corn Muffins

We got this idea from a cookbook titled *Superfoods: 300 Recipes for Foods That Heal Body and Mind*, by Dolores Riccio. Organized by ingredients, the recipes included in this book are accompanied by shopping, storage, and preparation tips and information about each food's benefits. Besides the recipes, it is a great reference book.

To make any muffins, of course, you must use a muffin tin with paper liners. Sometimes you can find the liners with seasonal designs (check your grocery's baking aisle). In our modification of this recipe, start with a premade mix for corn bread. Prepare it and bake it according to the directions on the box—except, of course, you'll be using a muffin tin. Before you spoon the batter into the liners, add a cup of blueberries to the mix. These are better fresh than canned, but if you do use canned berries, drain them thoroughly first.

If you're using these in Cakes and Ale, consider making mini-muffins. If you can time your baking so your muffins are still warm when you serve them in Circle, that's great, but if you can't, they're good at room (or Circle) temperature too.

Green Cabbage With Mushrooms

Cabbage is really good for you—full of what Dr. Andrew Weil, author of *Eating Well for Optimum Health*, calls "micronutrients." There are four types of these: vitamins, minerals, fiber, and protective phytochemicals. "Deficiencies of some of these dietary elements," Dr. Weil says, "will result in certain sickness and death, and of others in impairment of the body's defenses and suboptimal functioning of many of its systems." Cabbage won't save you from every dietary peril, but it'll help!

Cabbage and mushrooms are both good at Lammas too. Cabbage is a root vegetable, which makes it kind of wintry, but it's also nice and green like the Summer that is passing. Mushrooms are very autumny, and they remind us of the woods, and of basements and cellars where our Winter stores are kept.

Start with 1 small green cabbage (cored and diced, you should have about 6 cups), 1 medium-size onion (diced), and a 1/2 pound of mushrooms (sliced). (Oyster or shiitake mushrooms are best, but regular button mushrooms will do. If you really like mushrooms, use more than a 1/2 pound.) You will also need about 1 cup of vegetable stock (you can make your own or use canned).

Steam the cabbage in the stock for 5 minutes. When it just starts to wilt but is still bright green, take it off the heat and remove the cover from the pot. Leave the cabbage to keep cooking in the leftover heat. In a separate pan, sauté the onion and the mushrooms until they are brown. (Weil's recipe calls for you to sauté them in olive oil, but we use cooking spray.) When the onion and mushrooms are brown, add the cabbage. You may need to add a little of the vegetable stock—don't let it burn. Seasonings you can use include salt, pepper, dill, and paprika. Use margarine, sour cream, or even a couple of tablespoons of fat-free plain yogurt to dress up individual servings.

Salmon

Salmon is a sacred fish, associated with knowledge and wisdom. This makes it ideal for Sabbat tables. One of our favorites is a recipe that my husband found in our paper's advertising section, and we have been enjoying it for several years now (yet not too long, for the paper's not yellowed yet).

To begin, you will need 1 pound of salmon fillet, 2 cloves of garlic (minced), 1 teaspoon of lemon pepper, 4 thin slices of onion, 1/4 cup of white wine, 1 teaspoon of olive oil, 1/4 teaspoon of salt, and 1/2 lemon (sliced thin). Place the fillet in a dish, and combine the other ingredients in a bowl. Pour this mixture over the salmon, let it marinate for 20 minutes, and then bake it at 350° F (162° C) for 15 minutes, or until the fish flakes when you test it with a fork.

We like to serve this with rice and a green vegetable (green beans, peas, or Brussels sprouts, for instance).

ymbols

Bread

Loaves of bread are undoubtedly the most common symbols of Lammas—after all, *Lammas* means "loaf mass," referring to the honor given to the first loaf of bread made from the first grains of the season harvested.

We speak of "breaking bread," of sharing with our community, and by this we mean not just sharing the bounty of harvest, but also the work of harvest. It's not uncommon when we talk about sharing work and its rewards to hear the story of the Little Red Hen, who couldn't get the help she wanted with her bread-making, and, therefore, didn't want to share her bread. It's a parable meant to be taken literally, but literally is not the only way Wiccans understand things.

The Wiccan perspective includes the ideas that all sorts of work contributes to a goal, and the work we're doing isn't the only work that's worthy. We can't expect that everyone we know, much less those people we don't know well, will share our visions or agree with us about the best way to do things we all agree need doing. But Wicca finds strength in diversity. Our communities (certainly the Neo-Pagan community, and I'm personally sure the wider global community) would be the poorer if we all worked in just the same way toward the same goals.

Think for a moment what happens when everybody brings the same dish to a potluck. It might be interesting, for a few minutes, to explore the differences in the recipes. But you wouldn't have a balanced meal, and, eventually, you'd miss the dishes nobody brought. If everybody brings something different, maybe you will get to try something new. And what if somebody brings a dish that you can't or don't want to eat? You don't have to, no one is offended, and there is *still* plenty of other dishes for you to eat. This is a great start to any harvest, and, amazingly enough, a simple loaf of Lammas bread symbolizes all that.

A couple of other things I'd like to point out about bread are that every culture has some and finds it symbolic in some way, and that there are lots of kinds of it. Different cultures, of course, account for some of the different kinds of bread—what types of grain grow where you live will have a lot to do with what your bread is like. But even when the grain choice is limited, bread can either be whole grain or made from more refined flour, and it can contain ingredients beyond the basics that make it bread. Nuts, fruit, veggies—bread can be a simple transformation of grain, or it can incorporate just about the whole harvest!

Just as our harvests are of more than grain, not all bread is made from grain. My husband and I recently had the opportunity to taste dinner rolls made from taro (a potato-like root that is a Hawaiian staple) while on vacation. The rolls were sweet and a lovely shade of light purple, which certainly broke the ice at our table. We also brought home some taro pancake mix, which we're saving for this year's Mabon breakfast. Eating our purple pancakes will remind us—and reading this can remind you—that we can break bread with people who aren't sitting at the same table. It's hard to find a lot of major similarities between the Polynesian culture and the Celtic, but the concept of harvest and of enhancing our personal harvests by enlarging our sense of family/tribe to include more of the world(s) is one of them.

Braids

Lammas breads are often braided breads, and we can associate any braid with the Triple Goddess, whose cyclical renewal mirrors the process of death and rebirth. We can also understand the braid to represent the planting, growing, and harvest seasons, and the rain, sunlight, and earth that contribute to the grain's growth. Quite frequently, the breads with which we celebrate Lammas are seeded breads. (Faerie Moon, once a member of my coven, made the most wonderful poppy-seed bread I've ever had.) Obviously, the seed symbolizes the God's coming rebirth: He dies in His grain aspect to become the bread that keeps us alive, but the promise of His rebirth is in the seed. By eating the seed, we involve ourselves in that promise, not only committing ourselves to our part (planting) in His rebirth, but acknowledging that we will share in that rebirth.

Corn and Grain

The main ingredients of bread, corn and grain, also symbolize Lammas. "Corn and grain, corn and grain," we sing, "all that falls shall rise again." Other annuals, wild and decorative, also die in the Autumn (which begins at Lammas) and are reborn in the Spring. But in grains, this process is even more precious. Grains keep us alive when game is not available. Grain was once wild (and some still is), and domesticating it was one of humanity's most significant achievements.

As you know by now, I live in the Southwest. I'm not so familiar with fields of wheat or corn that grow as high as an elephant's eye; my "sense," if you will, of corn is influenced by Native tales of the Corn Maiden. She's an aspect of what Paula Gunn Allen, in *The Sacred Hoop: Recovering the Feminine in American Indian Traditions*, calls the quintessential spirit that pervades everything. The Corn Mother is a Gate-guardian for some Native cultures. Certainly the domestication of grains and grasses was humanity's gateway to permanent settlement, making it possible to wait for the game to come back, rather than having to pack up and follow it. Even in this way, "corn and grain" help us to focus on the cyclical nature of life!

The Full Moon

At first, it might surprise you to think that a full Moon is a symbol of Lammas: Wiccans celebrate full Moons as Esbats, and Esbats complement Sabbats as the Moon complements the Sun. But if you think about it just a minute longer, you'll realize that the August and September full Moons are *harvest* Moons. This is the time of year when we can see in real life that ever-so-romantic image of a stook of grain silhouetted against the golden Moon, and the time we also notice the equally romantic silhouettes of hawks gliding across an early-rising or late-setting Moon—though it's less romantic to see them capturing the field mice and other wee beasties they're hunting!

That image, of wheat or corn silhouetted against the full Moon, is what we might call a "comfort image" in our Western culture, and people from all over the Western world find that it can remind them of home. Wicca is, in fact, full of such images, and maybe that's one reason it's a growing religion. Wicca is not a superficial or sentimental religion, though, and there's deeper meaning to our symbols. What does the Moon mean to us? Let's consider some of the significance a full Moon has to Lammas.

First, the Moon is a symbol of the Goddess. The full Moon represents Her Mother aspect, so the full Moon as a symbol of Lammas can remind us of that potent mixture of grief and pride that any mother feels when she recognizes that her child's life has been given to a worthy cause. At the same time she understands and grieves the fact that she'll never see her child in that mortal form again, she also knows that the energy of her child's life now nurtures life in other ways. The mother also knows that even if there are no grandchildren carrying on her child's genetic legacy, her child's quest lives on in the others who share the same interests and who express the same passions.

Grief's darkness is not easily lightened, though, even by the full Moon and the Goddess's Mother aspect. It does sometimes happen that a harvest fails, succumbs to storm, pestilence, or vandalism, and it can be devastating. Lammas may also be a reminder of the rage a mother might carry when she feels her child's life has been taken in vain, the depression any of us can experience when we perceive our "harvest" as wasted. Wiccan thealogy neither diminishes our grief and anger, nor does it blame us for a spoiled harvest. If we are responsible, we're not to blame; rather, we are able to respond—creatively, even from the depths of despair. The full Moon at Lammas is a reminder that the Goddess suffers all that we do, and that we can recover joy as She does.

Whether we are ready to notice or not, the full Moon lights the night. It doesn't reveal details, but it gives us a silvered view of the major features of the land, and symbolically, of our subconscious minds by shining on the landscape of our souls. The full Moon's light is enough to get us from one side of the field to the other—enough to let us lengthen the day and keep at the physical work of harvest. In the light of a full Moon, we can work with cool heads, and as we all know, "cooler heads prevail."

In this light, we must find ways to distinguish ripe ears, bolls, and kernels without being able to see color and other details. Moonlight gives us an opportunity to "see" with other senses than our eyes, and that effort not only hones our survival skills, but it also refreshes us spiritually. Under the Moon, the Veil Between the Worlds is not such a solid barrier as it can seem to be in sunlight; what we cannot do is less obvious.

When we take advantage of the full Moon to work fields of stalk and furrow at night, we're still focused on picking, cutting, and the other physical work of the harvest. But when we're considering our nonagricultural harvests, the progress we've made toward our personal goals whether they be material or spiritual, the full Moon's light shows us perspectives we might not see by the light of day or by the light of culture.

Because our personal harvests are so all-encompassing, it's important that we assess and approach them from every angle, so the full Moon's symbolism of a mother's love and pride, a mother's support of our letting go of what we must for our own greater good, and its symbolizim of what Starhawk calls a "starlight" perspective on our lives, goals, and movement toward our goals, is imporant to remember and explore.

Games

Games also symbolize Lammas, although they come to mind more easily when we use the Sabbat's other name, Lughnassadh. Races and tests of strength are especially associated with this Sabbat, and not only because of the games Lugh established in honor of his foster mother. Tests of strength come in other forms—anyone who has kneaded their Lammas bread by hand can attest to that!

The Sun has been waning since Litha, and now we've begun to notice the shortening of the days and, in many places, the chilling of the nights. Faith that the Wheel is ever-turning, even here in Arizona where we're often yearning for Winter by mid-June, we're sorry to see the Summer's glory fade. Although we always hope for a good monsoon (a healthy start to Winter's respite from our famous dry heat), our indulgence in outdoor living increases—partly because the rains delight us so, but partly because we thrive on the heat that is so vital to all of life.

Wiccans accept that the God must die: He has, after all, ceded the Year at Litha, and without death, the promise of rebirth can't be fulfilled. And yet, even as His vitality spirals away southward in the sky toward Winter, we want to celebrate His strengths and we want to give Him and ourselves visible signs of our confidence that although He dies now, He will be restored. And so we make shows of vigor and prowess: We stage races and other shows of strength and endurance. Exercise releases endorphins that can relieve depression, and the reassurance these exhilarating activities give us is part of our harvest, part of what will carry us through the Winter.

Strawberries

Strawberries are among the modern symbols of Lammas. Other berries can also be representative of Lammas, and any fruits that grow wild where you live and ripen at the beginning of Autumn are appropriate to grace your altar and your feast table at Lammas. Corn bread and strawberries are our traditional Lammas Cakes, and sometimes someone brings extra strawberries with chocolate to dip them in! I'm one of many Wiccan Priestesses who acknowledges chocolate as sacred (as it really was to the Aztecs), so I'm happy to include it as part of any Sabbat feast.

Some flowers are edible, but, in many cases, the beautiful flower of a plant has to "die" so that the edible fruit can be "born." I use those words in quotes not only because the birth of a fruit isn't much like animal birth, but also because death isn't really death as we've been taught to understand it. It is a transformation. Gardeners do talk about "deadheading" spent blossoms, but we don't usually talk about blackberry flowers, for instance, "dying" when the bush begins to produce fruit. Rather, we speak of "fruiting" as being the bush's next activity. There's a cycle happening here—a progression, a transformation. Strawberries, and other berries, represent Lammas not only because they're ripe during this season, but also because they demonstrate the transformation that Lammas (along with all the other harvest Sabbats) is about.

Mabon

Some Wiccans liken Mabon to the secular American Thanksgiving. This is a useful comparison when non-Pagan friends need reassuring, but it's an oversimplification at best. Every Sabbat celebration contains an element of thanksgiving—we're always appreciative of being part of the cycle of life and to share a Circle with each other, the Quarters, and our Gods. The reason some of us correspond Mabon more particularly with Thanksgiving is that Mabon is Wicca's main harvest festival, often celebrated with cornucopias of fruit, bread, and vegetables.

Many Traditions of Wicca count the God as actually dying—finishing the process begun at Litha and continued through Lammas—at Mabon. As the fields are harvested and plowed under, so the God is buried. The return of His grain-body to the earth nourishes the soil, helping to make it fertile for next Spring's planting (of His own seed), and the bread and ale made from the grains that are harvested help keep us and our animals alive through the fallow Winter. His body thus usefully disposed of, His spirit returns (as do ours) to the Mother, through whom His solar aspect will be reborn at Yule.

Thus, at Mabon, we don't so much *mourn* His death as we do *acknowledge* His death (and ours too) as a step toward rebirth, which we celebrate. It's sad to see the forms change—amber waves of grain are movingly beautiful, as all healthy fields and meadows are—but change is growth, and growth is life. At Mabon we can understand death as growth, as part of the process of life, and so our cries of grief become shouts of celebration. As grain falls to the scythe, so it rises again in the oven as it becomes bread. The oven is another aspect of the grave, the womb, and the bread and ale of harvest are other aspects of the God, more forms in which we recognize and honor Him.

When I say that the process of the God's death is "finished" at Mabon, I don't really mean to say that it is *final*. That is, although the stalks, fruits, and vines in which the God has lived are finally cut in the harvest, and while those individual manifestations of the God will live no more in that form, no death is ever final. This is because death is only a stage in a process, and the harvest is only a stage within a stage. Something else we acknowledge at Mabon is that this death of the ripe outward forms of life that constitute our harvest, begins a transformative stage in the cycle of life.

It's not just that the fields begin their transformation from exhaustion to freshness as the spent stalks and leaves that have grown there release their nutrients back into the soil (and the "waste products" from other fields are added too). It's not just that the harvested grains, fruits, and other crops are prepared to feed us and our beasties through the coming Winter. Beyond these physical expressions of the process, the God's spirit returns to the wholeness that is the Goddess, and is reconstituted in the Elements of the Mother. By Samhain, He's taken a new form, a nonphysical form, and awaits His first rebirth at Yule.

We take part in this spiritual transformation whenever we eat and drink—and, yes, although it is not the least bit romantic, whenever we... return the byproducts of eating and drinking to the earth. Think about it. Whatever we eat was once alive, was once animate at some level of being, even if it didn't walk around and blink its eyes. It's not just the caloric energy of a plant or animal we take in at our meals, it's also the psycho-spiritual energy to which it gave form.

As Wiccans, I think it's our responsibility to give this a little more consideration than I suspect most of us usually do. We sometimes still joke about the idea that "you are what you eat," and when we do take it seriously these days, it's in terms of saturated fat, cholesterol, and carbs. All of this is definitely important, but it's also quite impersonal with respect to what we're eating. So beyond that, I think that "you are what you eat" needs to be understood in much the same way we interpret the idea that you need to "walk a mile" in someone else's shoes. And we need to take ideas such as "form follows function" into consideration too.

Bear with me and I'll make better sense of this. We know that our brains have developed to use both empirical and intuitive information, and we've discovered that the two sides of the human brain each specialize in one of these two modes of knowing. We can fairly conclude that we're meant to use both forms of knowledge, combining them into something more useful than either by itself, because our brains come with both sides connected. And we know that, individually, we learn best in various ways: some by reading, some by hearing, some by watching, and some by doing, for example. This gives us, individually and as a species, a truly remarkable—and we might even mark it as awesome or miraculous—capacity to imagine and understand experience beyond that which is firsthand. This is part of the diversity that both sustains life and expresses life's joy in itself.

What does this have to do with the variety of food we eat? Well, as I see it, our capacities, abilities, and talents—individually, culturally, and "species-ly"—create for us responsibilities as well as opportunities. Thus, I think what being human means (or at least suggests) is that because we have the *ability* to appreciate the world from other perspectives than our own, we consequently have an *obligation* to appreciate the world from other perspectives than our own. At the very least, I think this means that we must acknowledge the needs of the other creatures and features that share life on this planet with us, and to make an effort not to preclude meeting their needs as we meet our own.

To be brutally pragmatic, if we make it impossible for the things we eat to grow as they're meant to, as they've evolved to, we diminish our own food supply. I suppose you could argue that you have the right to starve yourself to death or to poison yourself, but I can't see how any of us can argue that we have the right to make that decision for other peoples who might not believe as we do and who might not interpret the workings of the world(s) in the same way. I think the greater our understanding is—empirical or intuitive—of life's processes, the greater our obligation is to make sure we don't impede them. We can take advantage of plenty of developing opportunities without precluding older options. And if new opportunities do preclude older ways, then maybe they're not opportunities worth taking.

The Wiccan Rede is (deceptively) simple: *An ye harm none, do as ye will.* But our will isn't our "feel like" or "wanna," it's our deepest purpose, and the Rede implies that we can all realize our deepest purpose in life without doing harm. Harm is difficult to define, of course, and every Tradition gives different examples. Beyond the obvious definitions common in penal codes and the rules of etiquette, a good rule of thumb is not to make any choices for yourself that leave others without choice. So when we harvest our crops and our herds, or when, as most of us do, we sustain ourselves with harvests that others have made for us, we have to think about the consequences of our choices.

These choices range from whether to buy free-range fowl, fish, and meat or what comes from feedlot herds and farms, to how much of our personal bounty we can share and how and who we share it with. There are a lot of choices in between those examples, too, and they do not all have to do with food. Try to remember that the altar cloths, Tools, tablecloths, serving dishes, utensils, and flowers that grace your altar and your

dinner table are also harvest products—not to mention the robes and
other clothes you wear, and the grooming products you use, and the car
and its fuel that take you to the store, and so on.

So when we celebrate the harvest at Mabon, we are right to enjoy our
successes, our accomplishments, and the work we've done to enhance
our lives. We are right to enjoy pooling and sharing our resources with
our friends and our loved ones. But it's also appropriate to celebrate the
harvest in a much wider sense, and to be especially aware of our day-to-
day, breath-to-breath interactions that are a continuous cycle of harvest
and replanting. If you want to liken Mabon to the holiday of Thanksgiving, remember that even Thanksgiving is a bigger holiday and has deeper
meanings than our culture lets on.

Mabon is the name of a god, too. In Celtic mythology, He is the son
of Modron, the Great Mother. In Their story, She does mourn His death,
but She looks forward in joy to His rebirth. His "death" is his abduction
at the tender age of 3 days, when He's imprisoned inside a stone wall. His
"rebirth" occurs when He is released from this wall, one of a number of
tasks a young man and his friends must accomplish in order for the young
man to gain permission to marry his sweetheart. Upon His release, Mabon
joins his rescuers and helps them complete their quest. (See the section
about Mabon lore.)

This is another way of telling the truth that harvest is work for many
hands, and that communities are nurtured and nourished in more ways
than one. Death isn't always the absence of life, rebirth is not always as
literal as we Wiccans find it at Yule or Imbolc, and harvest isn't always
about crops. In fact, in Wiccan cosmology, death is really never the absence of life, rebirth is really never physical in the mundane sense, and
harvest is always about a lot more than crops.

As we've just discussed, we give thanks for more at Mabon than just
the availability of food for the Winter. We give thanks for more than
just having a place to live and a job—we who have those things are
thankful for them every single day! If we're comparing Mabon to Thanksgiving, then, religiously, what Wiccans are thankful for at this season is
that we're part of The Process. I mean the natural process, which is actually a symphony of many processes. I mean, we are thankful to be dancing
the Spiral Dance. We are thankful (to summarize so we do not spend
hours trying not to leave anything out) to be carried along with the Wheel
as it rolls through the years of our lives.

Mabon follows Lammas, which begins our harvest season, and which, for most Wiccans, focuses on "first fruits." We can take this literally, of course, and be talking about apples (I, for one, can hardly wait until it's cool enough to use the oven and make the first apple crisp of the year). Or we can think about the "fruits" of our labor. This lets us consider our personal accomplishments as part of the harvest, which is certainly fair. Fairness can suggest balance, and personal harvests (such as quitting smoking or finishing a project on your house) balance the civic harvests we help bring in (such as going to work every day and doing the household shopping). If we want to play with words and concepts a little more, we can think about the harvest fairs. Then, we can consider our personal fairs, those being the ways we choose to share our harvests with family, friends, and the wider community.

Mabon is followed by Samhain, the season when we widen our communities to include our ancestors—our beloved dead. Samhain is also the time when we can consider our harvests, both personal and communal, in terms of history, of the past and future. The past nourishes the present, and the present nourishes the future. We each have personal pasts, and we all look forward to personal futures, of course. But we are also influenced by time before our remembering and will influence time beyond our experience. We can fail to appreciate our involvement in the cycle of life, but we can't really opt out; there's nowhere else to be, and harvest Sabbats are when this is made plainest to us.

We are—Canyondancer and I are at least, and I hope you are too—thankful to understand the world the way we do; to know that the Goddess and God are partners, not adversaries, and to know that matter and spirit are equally real and worthy. We are thankful to understand the "small-*e*" elements—rain, wind, sunlight, and snow—as gifts, not weapons of the Gods. We are thankful to understand the world's diversity—of plants, animals, landscapes, and cultures—as a strength, not a fault or threatening.

We are thankful that our liturgical material reassures us that we can all find fulfillment without destroying anyone else's chances of realizing their true will. We are thankful that Wicca's concept of personal responsibility remembers that none of us is the only person in this world, and that, sometimes, even if we've cleaned up after ourselves, we step in *other* people's karma. We are thankful that our Goddess has been with us from the beginning, and that we'll attain Her at the end of every incarnation. We are thankful that the Gods so obviously keep Their promises. We are thankful that our faith, while recorded in our *Books*, doesn't come from a book, but from the seasons that we celebrate.

And to whom are we thankful? Easy enough to say "the Gods," or "the Goddess and God," but who are They? Some Wiccans believe, as Druids do, that each sacred name identifies a distinct and individual goddess or god. More, I think, believe that each sacred name describes an aspect of the Great Goddess and Her Consort, the Horned God. After all, each of us has many names: Mom or Dad, Auntie or Uncle, for example. We are also identified by our patronym, occupational titles, and by where we live, our interests, our cultural heritage, and by our eccentricities. And let us not forget our Craft names, of which we may have more than one! All of our names and nicknames describe aspects of our personalities, but none of them does or can capture our wholeness, because names, words, and language are only meant to distinguish the details. It seems to me that the very act of talking about anything, gods included, requires us to be specific, even about things that are by nature more than specific.

The Adventure Tradition, which Canyondancer and I and our Initiates follow, teaches that on the physical plane humanity occupies, the Gods are natural forces, everything from gravity to photosynthesis, all that "astro/physics and chemistry stuff," and on the metaphysical plane, They are the Great Mother and the Horned God. She is all that is eternal and generative, and He is all that dies and is reborn, both really and symbolically.

I have felt the Gods's active presence in my life on several occasions, and I have sensed Their presence a few times more. I have never seen Them in any physical form, other than in the ways I think They commonly manifest: as woods and streams, as dappled sunlight, as birdsong, and as a doe's gentle nuzzle of her fawn, as selfless people acting heroically in the simplest of ways, as flowers insisting on blooming through cracked asphalt, and so on.

But I have seen Their Dance! I see it daily, as the cloud patterns pass my office window, and as the Sun rises and sets. I see it by the week, when from one Friday to the next I notice it getting dark a little earlier or a little later than usual. I see it by the month, as the trees in my yard grow green with buds or heavy with fruit, or surrender scent or leaf to the wind. I feel the temperature change as They sweep by me, waltzing 'round the Year as I've flown around more mundane dance floors.

I do not know Them as having faces, really, although I can represent Them that way. They have certainly touched me, but I do not know Them with hands. I have heard Them, but I do not know Them with lips or voices. I don't think They are diminished by the formulas with which I can name Them, and I do not think that They are more gloried when They're called by astral titles. I know that They go by and answer to all the names we call Them, just as each of us is known by many names and titles, for as multifaceted as we humans are, individually and as a species, They are more myriad.

They are, They dance, and this is as obvious to me as my own breath. In fact, my own breath is a step in the Dance, or a chord in its music, if you prefer—*and so is yours*. *To* this and *for* this I am thankful, in the sense that my awareness of it, my meditation upon it, causes great rejoicing in my heart. This is what I celebrate at Mabon.

Lore

The Sabbat of Mabon is named after the god Mabon. In Welsh legend, He's the Child of Light and the son of the Earth Mother Goddess, Modron. As Demeter grieves for Persephone's "abduction" (and by the way, many Wiccans prefer to reinterpret that story as being about initiation), Modron grieves because Mabon was taken from Her when He was only 3 days old!

In some stories, He's imprisoned in a stone wall at Caer Loyw, where His release is eventually won by the companions of Kilwich, a young suitor who is seeking the hand of a maiden named Olwen. These companions are helping Kilwich (sometimes spelled Culhwch) to accomplish the many formidable tasks set for him by Olwen's father, King Ysbaddaden—a Giant chieftain. Ysbaddaden's life was predicted to end when his daughter married, and Kilwich's particular problem was that he couldn't get married at all except to Olwen. (See the section about Litha lore.)

We can understand Mabon's disappearance and imprisonment, which loosely parallels other cultures' myths to explain Winter in terms of grief and loss. Perhaps the Child of Light's removal from His mother's joy symbolized a terrible crime against the Earth, or the Goddess, or motherhood in general, which was punished by months of unproductive cold and darkness. I don't deny that this may have made sense in other cultures and other times, but it seems to me that the idea of the Goddess making Her other children suffer for Her grief is inconsistent with Wiccan principles.

We could just as reasonably interpret Mabon's disappearance as initiatory; remember, He's a god, not a human, so there's no reason to imagine Him as helpless at 3 days old, as any of our children would be. In this case, the approaching Winter wouldn't be the Goddess's manifest grief. Rather, late Autumn and Winter's darkness would symbolize Mabon's inner journeying. His "imprisonment" in a stone wall (an aspect of the

Underworld) might be an acknowledgment of the difficulties any individual has when trying to get along alone; we're always alone on our inner journeys, even if our companions' wisdom helps to guide us.

When adventurers come along—led to Mabon by the oldest of all creatures, the Salmon, which still represents wisdom-from-knowledge—who are willing to risk themselves in battle to free him, Mabon rejoins the world. As the tale is told from Kilwich's perspective, it's the adventurers' daring that facilitates the rescue. But we shouldn't forget that Mabon had to be ready for and cooperative with their mission. Someone who hasn't gotten far enough along on the inner journey is as likely to perceive another obstacle as a band of rescuers!

In many senses then, it's both legitimate and fitting for Wiccans to interpret this tale as a demonstration of the balance we all need to find between individuality and wholeness, between self-sufficiency and reliance on community. Whether the considerations made in naming the Autumn Equinox on the Wheel of the Year after the god Mabon were consciously researched or not, given the way we can interpret what little we know of this god's experience makes it deeply appropriate. We can say He was "harvested" from the wall, we can say He "harvested" rescue from His personal journey, and we can say His rescue allowed Kilwich to complete the "harvest" of His destiny. All of these harvests represent social and psychological balance, which is just as important to any community as the literal harvesting of fields and the grace period that an Equinox's balance between seasons affords us.

Although many Celtic myths correspond beautifully with the meanings we now see in the seasons' change at the Autumn Equinox, "there's no historical basis," according to liturgist Kirk Thomas of Tucson's Sonoran Sunrise Grove of ADF Druids, for observing Mabon as a holiday. However, the Sonoran Sunrise Grove is likely to "use the Mabinogi and celebrate balance with the story of Manawydan and Pryderi, and the horde of mice. All is out of balance," he summarizes, "and then restored in the end."

For any who don't know or don't remember this story, I'll give it a short go here (also refer to a copy of the Mabinogi, or Welsh legends, which should be in every Wiccan's library as well as in every Druid's):

Pryderi is the son of Pwyll, King of the Underworld (which is also known as the Summerland, or at least a region of it), and Rhiannon, a Mother and Sovereignty goddess. Manawydan is Pryderi's stepfather (Rhiannon's second husband) in some versions, and Pryderi's cousin in others. The point is that there are strong clan obligations between them.

Manawydan's sister Branwen has been married to the King of Ireland, and there has been a bit of skullduggery going on in their court. It is with Manawydan's return from the consequent war with Ireland that the story about the mice begins. Manawydan is feasting with Pryderi, who has offered to arrange for him to marry Rhiannon. The first part of the adventure begins as they and their retinues are taking an after-dinner walk: There's a mighty thunderclap, after which a blinding mist surrounds them.

When it passes, everyone but Pryderi, his wife Kicva, Manawydan, and Rhiannon are gone. Reduced to hunting to survive, the men eventually flush a boar that spooks their dogs. They follow the boar to a castle that stands where neither remembers any building before. Although they suspect a trap, Pryderi goes in to make inquiries after his dogs. There's no one to ask, but he sees a magnificent fountain with a golden bowl suspended over it. When he touches it, it captures his hands and he can't let go. His feet are stuck to the marble floor, and he's struck dumb as well. Manawydan returns to Rhiannon and tells her about it, and she goes to rescue her son, but finds herself trapped in the same way.

Now Manawydan and Kicva travel to England where they become shoemakers—such good shoemakers that the others in town find their livelihoods threatened, so they decide to kill Manawydan and Kicva. The couple is warned, though, so they leave town before the plot can be carried out. They leave with a packet of wheat, which they sow in three fields when they get back to their own lands.

When the wheat in the first field comes ripe and Manawydan goes to harvest it, he discovers every ear of wheat had been cut and taken away and that there is nothing left but straw! He checks out the second field, and it too is ripe. But the next morning when he goes to harvest it, it too is gone, and nothing is left but more straw. So he decides to guard the third field that night to see what the heck is going on.

At midnight, he hears a rustle and sees a horde of mice, too many to count. Each mouse is chewing a single ear of wheat away from the stalk and carrying it off, leaving the third field full of straw. Furious, he runs after them, but catches only one. He takes it home, a prisoner in his glove, and tells Kicva he'll be hanging it the next morning for the thief it is. Thinking that this is just a bit undignified for a King of the Underworld, she tries to dissuade him, but he is not disposed to listen to her advice.

The next day happens to be the seventh anniversary of the day the mist came, in which all their companions were lost. As Manawydan is setting up a tiny gallows for the mouse, along comes an old man, a scholar. They chat a bit, and the scholar also advises Manawydan that taking revenge upon such a lowly creature is unseemly, but Manawydan will not let the mouse go. Some time later as he's completing his preparations to hang the wee beastie, an old Priest comes by and offers to buy the mouse, but Manawydan will not be deterred by a price or an argument, least of all an argument for his own dignity.

As the noose is tightening around the mouse's neck, a bishop approaches with his full retinue, and he too pleads with Manawydan to spare the mouse's life. Manawydan is at first unrelenting, but finally he is willing to negotiate. He asks for the freedom of Pryderi and Rhiannon (remember them, stuck to the fountain?) and the restoration of his kingdom in return for the small creature's life. He does want to know why the life of this mouse is so dear, and the bishop (I should say "bishop") tells Manawydan that the mouse is his wife.

Turns out the "bishop" is a man named Lloyd, a friend of a man named Gawl, for whose sake he took this seven-year vengeance on Pryderi. What had Pryderi done to Gawl in order for his friend to seek revenge? Well, nothing actually, except to be Rhiannon's son by Pwyll. Rhiannon had been promised to Gawl in marriage, but refused him on account of her love for Pwyll. Gawl had sworn not to take revenge for this slight, but his friends made no such oath.

So Manawydan promises to free Lloyd's wife, who is only a mouse by an enchantment devised to aid in Lloyd's revenge on Pryderi. But before doing so, Manawydan extracts a promise from Lloyd that there'll be no more of this wicked magic done, so order is indeed restored.

When you understand that Manawydan is a god of craftsmanship and agriculture, you see why it was his wheat that Lloyd assailed. If Manawydan's wheat won't grow, his authority over the land is diminished, if not negated altogether. His being Rhiannon's second husband puts him in Lloyd's sights, on Gawl's behalf too. But Gawl was rich and greedy, and insensitive to the woman he claimed to love and, by extension, no doubt to the land itself. Revenge taken on his behalf reflected the illegitimacy of his authority, too, and affected not merely the individual who had wronged him, but innocents as well.

Furthermore, though Lloyd didn't break a personal oath by taking revenge for Gawl, he certainly worsened Gawl's reputation, for Gawl had sworn not to seek revenge. Just as they're not fooled now, people weren't fooled then when powerful people disclaimed any responsibility for benefit resulting from what their pals and minions did. In the end, the revenge had to be withdrawn. Harvest and the natural way of things may not lightly be impinged, or, as we used to say, "It's not nice to fool Mother Nature."

The Asatru celebrate a *hausblot*, or Autumn harvest festival, on September 23. *Hausblot* may be translated as "house blessing," and that "house" traditionally means not only the dwelling, but the family as well. It reminds us that a harvest is about more than just gathering the crops and safely storing them before it freezes. Harvest is about reaffirmation of relationships and the obligations those relationships create for us.

And while many Wiccans are familiar with the Irish and Welsh lore associated with Mabon, many Wiccan celebrations of the harvest seasons focus on the harvest itself and the transformation of grain to an edible form. Our associations of Mabon with Thanksgiving highlight the other tangible forms of harvest too. None of us live by bread alone; science and intuition tell us that we need each other's nurture, and Wicca tells us that our care for each other is an important part of our harvest, too, materially and ritually.

ituals

The Tucson Area Wiccan-Pagan Network (T.A.W.N.) has been holding Mabon rituals that are open to the public since 1988. Before it retired and disbanded, my coven had the honor of presenting two of them. Every year, a different individual or group was responsible for organizing the Mabon rite, and so our community has been privileged to see a wide variety of Mabon rituals.

Though the Traditions represented and the styles demonstrated have varied widely, the main theme has always been the transformation of the harvest from growing grain to the community's sustenance. It's challenging to share Cakes and Ale with a large group, and the easiest way to meet that challenge is to assign one or two servers at each Quarter so that no one has to wait too long for the chalice or the plate to come around to them. The best way to avoid spreading germs is to serve the Ale (or Wine, you might call it) in small paper cups. Of course, in any public ritual, the Ale should be nonalcoholic. At Mabon, apple cider is a wonderfully appropriate substitute for spirited Ale.

As popular a theme as it is, the transformation of crop to bread is itself symbolic of the God's death and rebirth, and this can be depicted in ways that don't involve wheat sheaves or ears of corn, which some Wiccans like to reserve for Lammas celebrations. We mustn't forget that most of us don't live by bread alone, and Wiccans honor the God in His horned forms too. Although one of the following rituals emphasizes the crop transformation aspect of Mabon, another emphasizes the death of the Horned God, and our faith that He'll be reborn come Spring.

The Rite of the Corn God

My memory has conflated several Autumn festival rituals to produce this rite. I've simplified it, because you'll want to embellish it with your own ideas and according to your own or your group's talents and other resources. If your celebration is openly Wiccan, you'll be in a fully cast

Circle; if you're sharing this with non-Pagans, you may want to make it more folksy and less religious. You'll know which parts to emphasize, which to change, and which to leave out altogether as you modify this rite to suit your circumstances.

Set the altar at North or East, as suits you. You'll need a bowl or bag of popcorn (depending on the number of people celebrating) and some decorative ears of corn and/or stalks of wheat. If you cannot find real wheat, you can use plastic stalks that are available at most craft stores. You'll also need a large cauldron. Again, if you don't have a metal one, or a metal one big enough to hold both the popcorn and the decorative grain, you can use one of the plastic ones sold for Halloween. If no such thing is available to you, a cardboard box wrapped in black cloth will serve the purpose. Whatever you use, it should be at West. The popcorn should be ready in the cauldron, and the decorative grain should be on or under the altar where the Priest can reach it easily. A piece of black or brown cloth may be ready by the cauldron to make this rite more dramatic.

When the Circle has been cast (see Appendix A in *Celebrating the Seasons of Life: Samhain to Ostara* for casting directions), invoke the Gods:

> *Lady of the Corn, Queen of the Grain,*
> *we seek Your strength in harvest's pain.*
> *Your son's to the scythe, Your lover to blade,*
> *and You bereaved have been made.*
> *To You our arms now open wide:*
> *we share Your grief: our God has died.*
> *Be here with us, and not forlorn,*
> *for as You've taught us, He'll be reborn!*
> *Hail, Great Goddess, and welcome!*

> *Lord of the Corn, King of the Grain,*
> *we seek Your blessing through harvest's pain.*
> *You're down to scythe; they call You dead—*
> *will You live on in ale and bread?*
> *Be here with us in seed and feast,*
> *for to rebirth is grief released!*
> *Hail, Lord of the Grain, and welcome!*

As the clergy invoke, everyone else echoes the hails and welcomes. (Solitaries should repeat those lines, with uplifted arms the second time.) After a heartbeat's pause, a slow beat begins on drums, with clapping hands, stomping feet, or with rattles. To this beat (a solitary will keep slow time in his or her head), the Priest goes to the altar and picks up the decorative grain. He dances with the corn or wheat above his head (if you are a solitary woman, identify yourself as the God when you pick up the grain), spinning slowly as he progresses deosil around the Circle. He may wish to pick up the pace a bit in this part of his dance.

When he reaches South, he cries out something such as, "I am strong! I am ripe!" Simultaneously, he dances in place vigorously, with great leaps. Eventually, though, he begins to grow weary. He begins to make his way, more slowly now and lowering the grain he holds, to the West. By the time he gets there, he is moving slowly and stiffly. Perhaps he gives the corn or wheat a last shake or rattle over his head in memory of his Summer vitality, or perhaps he dances jiggishly in place with one last burst of energy.

Then the Priestess comes to him and says, "My lord, it is time." She may take the grain from his hands and put it in the cauldron, or she may guide his hands as he lays it there himself. He will then kneel beside the cauldron. If you are using a dark cloth in this rite, the Priestess covers his head with it, and if the setup allows, he lowers himself to the ground and lays there, still, for a few moments. All the while, the rhythm is maintained by the rest of the celebrants.

For a moment, the Priestess bows over the fallen Priest/God in grief, and then she stands and turns inward to face everyone in the Circle. She dries her eyes and, clapping her hands, joins in the rhythm, and begins to speed it up a little. When the energy begins to rise, she says, "The God has died, yet He has *not* died! He is among us still!" While the livelier rhythm continues, she reaches into the cauldron and pulls out the bag of popcorn, and holds it over her head as if it's a trophy she is showing off. As she does this, she nudges the Priest with her toe, and he too rises, throwing off the cloth if he is covered by one.

The Priestess lowers her arms and the Priest feeds her a bite of the popcorn, saying, "May you never hunger." She then feeds him a bite, repeating the same words. Next, they toss a few bits of popcorn into the air as they take the bag around and offer it to everyone present.

When everyone has had some popcorn, the bag is set down at the base of the altar and the Priest and Priestess proceed to consecrate the Ale, which they share as well. After that, the Circle proceeds in the "usual way" until it is closed.

For some people, this will represent a reversal in the conduct of Cakes and Ale: In many Traditions, the Ale is consecrated and shared first. On top of that, in this ritual, the popcorn is a substitute for the more conventional "Cake," and it's not formally consecrated. The transformation of the grain from the altar into the popcorn, the demonstration of the God's immortality by His life's transformation, is consecration enough for this rite. To interrupt the drama would distract us from it, and that would be unsuitable, so the consecration of the Ale waits. (Besides, grain in its preparation is ready to make bread, which the popcorn also symbolizes, before it's ready to make ale.)

It would, of course, be possible to substitute crackers for popcorn, and this might be appropriate if the Priest is carrying a sheaf of wheat around the Circle. Popcorn, however, is usually more fun, and I think it's the best choice if children are present, no matter what grains you use to represent the harvest.

How the Priest and Priestess who stand for the God and Goddess are costumed, how and how long the Priest/God dances, how participatory the dance is, what instruments are played to keep time, and the exact words the Priest/God and Priestess/Goddess say are up to the individuals and covens performing the ritual. When the rite is held is also a matter of choice, although dusk is the time of day that corresponds to this Sabbat.

Finally, to thank the Gods, say:

> *Lady of the Corn, Queen of the Grain,*
> *we found Your strength in harvest's pain.*
> *Your son was to scythe, Your lover to blade,*
> *and You bereaved had been made.*
> *To us Your arms were open wide:*
> *we shared Your grief: our God had died.*
> *Yet here You came, and we were none forlorn,*
> *and we witnessed together the God reborn!*
> *Hail, Great Goddess, and farewell!*

Lord of the Corn, King of the Grain,
Your blessing's received, and harvest made gain.
You were down to scythe; they called You dead,
yet You lived on in ale and bread!
And here You were, in seed and feast,
and to rebirth was our grief released!
Hail, Lord of the Grain, and farewell!

The Rite of the Horned God

This rite is more somber than the Rite of the Corn God, and it requires a bit more imagination from the participants; it relies a little more on the delayed gratification aspect of faith. In addition to a normal altar setup (North or East, according to your custom and preference), you'll need a dark-colored bandanna (any design is fine as long as it's a dark color), an antler headdress, and a dark cape for the Priest to wear.

If you don't have a dark cape, then a dark piece of cloth, a dark hooded coat, or even a dark-colored couch throw, bedspread, or sheet will do. If you really can't find anything to use as a cape or cloak, find or make a dark mask for the Priest to wear (it should cover his whole face, not just his eyes). The bandanna and the dark cloth (or mask) should be folded or set unobtrusively at West. (If you're using a mask instead of a cloak, you will not need a bandanna. If you have a cloak, you will still need a bandanna.)

Another option is to include a horn in this rite. A horn is an enriching accessory if one is available. The little tin ones sold to celebrate the secular New Year will work, and the sound of a medieval hunting horn can also be imitated by voice.

In this rite, you may want to use strips of jerky for Cakes (or use them in addition to more traditional Cakes). This alternative is appropriate because the God's horned aspect—usually a stag—is honored in this rite, and jerky is a little more representative of the Horned God than Cakes, which are made of grains. If you choose to represent the God's offering of His life as nourishment in this way, be sure there's one strip for each person present.

If you are a solitary performing this rite, you will have to take all the parts yourself. Because of this, you may prefer to rewrite some portions of this ceremony to make it easier. You could, for instance, turn the

Goddess's lines into narration so that your characterization of the God is not completely interrupted (this would be the most appropriate option for male solitaries). If you're doing it by yourself, you may want to use a tape recorder for "sound effects," such as the hunting horn, or for background music to give the rite a little of the texture that more people would provide.

When the Circle is cast, invoke the Gods like this:

> *Lady of the Wood, Underworld Queen,*
> *show us what good from death we can glean.*
> *Your son's to the arrow, Your lover to blade,*
> *and You bereaved have been made.*
> *To You our arms now open wide:*
> *we share Your grief: our God has died.*
> *Be here with us, and not forlorn,*
> *for as You've taught us, He'll be reborn!*
> *Hail, Great Goddess, and welcome!*

> *Lord of the Wood, Slayer and Slain,*
> *You offer us life through the hunt's death and pain.*
> *You're down to the arrow; they call You dead—*
> *yet You call us to see this fate without dread.*
> *Ho! Be with us now as we toast the feast,*
> *for to rebirth is grief released!*
> *Hail, Horned God, and welcome!*

If there are several people present, they should begin a drummed or clapped rhythm. If there is a horn, it should be sounded (or someone can imitate the sound) to signal that the "hunt" has begun. This ritual doesn't enact a realistic hunt in that there is no Hunter, but the Priest will now strap on the antlers (he now represents the Horned God), and he will "dance" around the Circle as though he is a stag pursued by a hunter.

This dance should proceed largely widdershins (counterclockwise), though some deosil (clockwise) movement can be included. There should be as much head-tossing as the headpiece will allow. There should also be much dipping of the shoulders, combined with the occasional straightening and arching of the back as the hunted stag sniffs the air, and in it, his doom. Rattles in the hands of other coveners might sound like rustling bushes. Once or twice someone might cry out, "There he is!" As long as it doesn't become comical—there's a time and a place for mirth, and this isn't it—even the sound of hunting dogs' yips can be added.

When the energy is suitably high, the Priestess signals the Priest to stagger as if hit by a hunter's arrow. He then dies dramatically, falling to the ground at West. The hunting horn is sounded again (or the sound of a horn is made by one of the coveners), and all the clapping and drumming stops. In silence, the Priestess covers the Priest/God's body, the fallen stag, with the dark cloak or cloth, and puts the bandanna in his hand. If there is no dark cloak or cloth, the Priestess should spread her arms over the Priest as if she's covering his fallen body, and screen him with the skirts of her robe if he needs to realign himself so that his head is facing away from the Circle. She should also make sure he has the mask in his hand instead of the bandanna. The horn is then sounded again.

The Priestess restarts the drumming or clapping while, under his "shroud," the Priest removes his antlers and rises, covering his head and face with the cloak or cloth. If there is no cloak or cloth, he should don the mask as invisibly as possible. The Priestess may do a little dance of her own, with exaggerated gestures of grief and weeping, to distract the coven from the Priest's costume change.

When he is ready, the Priest rises again, his face hidden, his body crouched and hunched, for now he has died and is making his journey through the Underworld. He makes his way slowly, to the rhythm clapped or drummed by the coven, toward the altar. As the Priest moves through the Underworld between West and North, the Priestess moves deosil to the altar, where she stands to watch the Priest play out the God's journey. When he reaches the altar, the Priest, his face still covered by the cloak or cloth, unfurls his bandanna and places it over the plate of Cakes. If he is masked instead of cloaked, keeping his face turned away from everyone, he should remove his mask and cover the Cakes with it.

If the altar is at East, the Priest/God makes a short deosil turn back toward North. Once at North, he discreetly cuts a very small Door and steps just outside the Circle, where he hunches down with his back toward the Circle. He holds this position for one or two heartbeats, and then, still hunched over, he turns in place to face the Circle again. He does not rise, and he keeps his head down (unless he is cloaked, in which case he makes sure the cloak is covering his face before he raises his head at all). To symbolize the transition the God will make from death to life, he then spreads his arms wide, palms toward the Circle.

His gesture is the cue for the Priestess to take "the Goddess position," standing with her legs spread and her arms outstretched, facing the Priest. She, too, holds the position for a moment, and then slowly turns toward the altar. With both hands, she lifts the God's bandanna or mask away from the Cakes, and holds it up for a moment before she lays it down beneath the altar. Then, she raises the plate of Cakes to show it off. She says:

> *The God is gone, yet is not gone;*
> *His death is but transition.*
> *Till He is back with us anon,*
> *His life is our nutrition!*

She sets the plate of Cakes back on the altar, and moving deosil around the Circle if the altar is at East, she comes to North and cuts a Door for the Priest, who throws off the cloak (if he's wearing one), and stands up to become himself again. He reenters the Circle through the Door cut for him, and joins the Priestess at the altar to proceed with the normal consecration of Cakes and Ale. The Circle concludes as usual when Cakes and Ale have been shared.

If you are using jerky as part of the rite of Cakes and Ale, everyone present should take a piece and raise it as if raising a glass to make a toast and say, "Hail the Horned God!" They should then take a bite in unison. Whether to finish the jerky strip before you carry on with the rest of Cakes and Ale or set it aside until the Ale has been consecrated is up to you. (The Priest already consecrated the Cakes with the God's energy when he covered them with his bandanna or mask.)

Mabon Vow

At Mabon, the Year is balanced, just as it is at Ostara, between Summer and Winter. At Mabon, the balance is tipped toward Winter. The points I made about balance when I discussed Ostara in this book's sister volume (*Celebrating the Seasons of Life: Samhain to Ostara*) are valid at Mabon, too, but as the seasons' flow carries us toward Winter, the examples that come to my mind are different.

At this time of year, the best examples I can give of balance in context have to do with the balancing acts I do in my storeroom when I'm digging through seasonal decorations to find the cornucopia. My storeroom holds not only drawers, shelves, and boxes full of "stuff," but also lots of empty boxes that I "might need" one day. Full boxes are better for balancing other full boxes on, and while that's undoubtedly true figuratively, it's a practical observation offered from experience. (Balance is easier to achieve when you're not trying to keep cats from pouncing on you or the things poking out of the boxes, too.)

Whenever I go through the storeroom, looking for places to keep the bits and pieces I've accumulated through the Summer—crafts, materials for crafts, souvenirs of trips, gifts I've bought in advance of Yule, etc.—I'm always inclined to sort through what's already in there and get rid of what I can. Sometimes I have to get rid of some things in order to make room for what I want to bring in. (A principle of O'Gaea's Theory of Housework, as articulated by Canyondancer, is that it's easier to get rid of something than to actually put it away.)

When we think of harvest, we think mostly of "bringing in." However, let me use a sort of agricultural example: If you've only got one barn, its storage space is not infinite. If you don't want to waste this year's yield, you may well have to take some of last year's hoard out and use it, give it away, or offer it back to Nature more directly in order to find room for what's waiting outside in the wagons or bags you just filled. In other words, harvest involves a winnowing beyond that which we do as part of preparing this year's grain to mill or amass. Harvest itself involves a certain amount of balancing.

When we say "the hand that holds the scythe transforms," we're not just talking about cutting down the stalks of grain or slaughtering the livestock, although those literal uses of the blade certainly are transformative. But taking "scythe" more figuratively, we can see that deciding what to keep and what to cast away—what grain to save for making bread and what to use for seed, what provisions to stash in the pantry and what to put out on the table to share, or what things you "might need" to pass along to make room for things you know you'll use—is an important part of harvest work too.

Of course, we don't need to be talking about physical things at all. All of this is true about things we were told, perhaps as gospel, perhaps in jest, perhaps without intent at all, that we still believe about the world even though they contradict our experience or fail to meet our needs. A crucial element of any harvest is rejecting the grain gone bad, lest it contaminates the lot and leaves you without staple sustenance for the Winter. (It's both metaphorically and literally true, we have recently learned, that you shouldn't use downer cows as feed for a healthy herd. Leaving aside the "forced cannibalism" issue, we've seen through past cases of mad cow disease that a little more attention to the whole work of harvest would have saved a number of herds, and perhaps some meat-eaters' nerves.)

Take Mabon's vow when you're ready to wield the scythe not only in your garden, but in your inner fields. You may want to have handy a representation on paper of some "contaminated" or "unhealthy" attitude or habit that you need to be rid of. Cut it up and dispose of the pieces to symbolize your readiness, the room in your heart and mind, for a healthier harvest that can be relied upon to nourish you this Winter.

The Wheel turns on—'tis Mabon-tide.
Dawn and dusk abreast now ride
darkness, brightness, calm and storms.
The hand that holds the scythe transforms.
I vow this wisdom shall be my own:
poise will let my power be known.
From balance the Wheel now turns toward the deep.
Through Winter, by vow and faith, I'll keep.

ctivities

Harvesting your own garden is an ideal Mabon activity. If you can, display your produce, whether it's edible or not, in a basket on your altar. If you don't have a garden, you can create one to harvest.

For one of our Lammas rituals, we made rows of wheat. For a Mabon harvest rite, you can use that wheat again or make other paper crops; line them up just as you did at Lammas, and harvest them again. You can also get silk veggies at your local craft store and set those out in rows. You might even be able to use some of the decorative garlands you already have on hand.

A Grape Harvest

You can easily make a vineyard. Use the cardboard tubes from rolls of wrapping paper as upright supports for the "vines" you'll make from construction paper. To keep the tubes standing up, make a base in the shape of a cross for each one. Cut slits into one end of each tube and slide it into a base in order to keep the tube upright. (See illustration.)

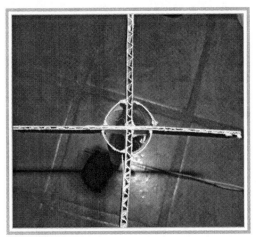

A view of the bottom of a cardboard vineyard stake shows the easy-to-create base that supports it.

String yarn or twine between two or three of the cardboard "stakes," and then make a vine, stems, leaves, and grapes out of brown, green, and purple construction paper. Tape your vine to the "stakes" and extend some grapes across the yarn strands, but don't overload them or the weight may collapse the stakes.

Ears of Corn

I learned this craft from Hearth's Gate Coven Priestess Chandra Nelson and her daughter Ivy, and it's doubly appropriate for Mabon because it in-volves popcorn! Making popcorn, of course, is symbolic of the way the God's death in the corn harvest be-comes our life when we eat the prod-ucts of the corn, of which popcorn is the most immediate. The first step of this craft is to make popcorn.

Another way to make a vineyard is with the tubes from rolls of wrapping paper and straightened wire hangers. This one is "ripe" with grapes (purchased from a craft store) hanging from paper clips. Hal the Kitty is helping with the harvest!

Canyondancer and I like to make popcorn the old-fashioned way: Heat oil in a covered pan, test its readiness with one or two kernels, and add more when they begin to pop. (You can find jars of ready-to-pop kernels in your local supermarket.) Make sure to keep shaking the pan on the stove so the corn doesn't burn. This may be labor-intensive and time-intensive, but the effort is only a fraction of what real farmers put into their crops and harvests. Anyway, no matter how you make your popcorn, be sure not to eat it all or you won't have enough left for this activity! (Don't salt or butter what you need for this craft either!)

Along with the popcorn, you will need white, beige, or yellow con-struction paper, green construction paper or tissue paper, and craft glue. Tape or staples and some white or yellow lengths of yarn are optional.

Using white, beige, or yellow construction paper, roll a cone for a cob. You can use glue to keep the cone's shape, but make sure you give it enough time to dry. If you don't want to wait, tape or staple the cone.

(If you use tape, use small pieces and as little as possible.) From green construction paper or tissue paper, cut long leaf-shaped pieces for the corn husks, and tuck them into the top of the cone. If you would like, use a few strands of yellow or white yarn for corn silk, and attach them to the inside of the cone. Now, glue pieces of popcorn to the cone.

Your finished "ears of corn" will be a wee bit fragile, but even with a few pieces of corn missing, they look neat, and if you make several, you can tie them together with lengths of yarn and use them for decoration. Save them carefully for a few weeks after Mabon, and you can use them again as part of your Thanksgiving decorations.

Decoupage Altar Cover

Even before Mabon, leaves are starting to turn color and fall in most places. Organize a field trip to a local park, or even your front yard or back-yard, to collect colorful leaves. Try to choose ones that are whole and as flat as possible, and as many as you think you will need to cover your altar. Do this several days before Mabon so you have time to dry them for at least a week. I like to do this by folding paper

With a little help from her mom, Chandra, Ivy Nelson-Thacker made this ear of corn for O'Gaea, who is keeping it for an annual Mabon and Thanksgiving decoration.

towels over them, placing them between the pages of big books, and then stacking more books on top to increase the weight. (Again, there are quicker ways to dry leaves, but I think it is best to do things at harvesttime in ways that take a little more time and effort, just like harvesting crops.)

When the leaves are flat and dry, glue them to a large piece of construction paper—any color will do, but the piece should be large enough to cover most of your altar without hanging over. Use undiluted glue to attach the leaves to the paper, but use a mixture of one part glue to one part water to achieve a decoupage effect. Paint this mixture over the leaves, fully covering the paper. Let it dry for several hours, and then apply another coat.

The more coats of decoupage mixture you layer over the leaves, the more protected your altar cover will be, and the more depth it will seem to have. If you have time to coat the altar cover with several layers, you can even add a few smaller leaves, some glitter, or other tiny decorations between some of the layers. Be sure the cover is completely dry before you use it on your altar.

Before you use it on your altar, you'll need to consecrate it, for all the Tools Wiccans use in a Circle are consecrated. Here's a consecration you can use for this cover, and another one for any other crafts you'll be using in your Mabon Circle:

Altar Cover Consecration

You creature of paper, leaf, and glue,
with holiness I now charge you.
I hail the paper, made from the tree;
I hail the leaf that falls in harvest colorfully.
I hail the glue, made too from death,
and hail rebirth that comes in faith.
I pledge you honor, respect, and care,
by Earth and Water, Fire and Air.
Now conjoined to guard and clothe,
be consecrated by this oath!

A Consecration for Altar Decorations

Made from things I buy or find,
by my hands, my faith to bind!
Earth and Water, Air and Fire,
transform these things familiar.
So blessed, these things I consecrate
for the Sabbat we celebrate!

Runes

In *Celebrating the Seasons of Life: Samhain to Ostara*, we looked at Runes pertaining to Ostara because that Sabbat is named after an Anglo-Saxon goddess, and the Anglo-Saxon Runes are part of Wicca's heritage. In this volume, we're looking at Runes related to Mabon because Mabon is across the Wheel from Ostara on Wicca's liturgical calendar. Mabon is our main harvest festival, too, and a good harvest has always been one of the main focuses of all sorts of magic, including Rune-magic.

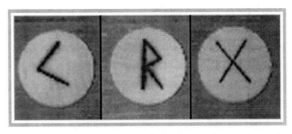

Examples (from left to right) of Cen (Kenaz), Rad (Raido), and Gifu (Gebo) from the author's set of Runes.

According to Freya Aswynn in *Leaves of Yggdrasil* [republished as *Northern Mysteries and Magick: Runes, Gods, and Feminine Powers* (Llewellyn Publications, 1998)], Cen, Rad, and Gifu (known in the Elder Futhark as Kenaz, Raido, and Gebo) are associated with Mabon. Let's take a brief look at those Runes. (To my Asatru readers, let me say that I do not claim any deep knowledge of the Runes. Instead, I have a great respect for their wisdom and power. My purpose in exploring them in this book is to demonstrate a relationship between Asatru and Wicca, and to encourage readers to further study both the Runes *and* Asatru.)

Cen (pronounced *ken*) stands for a torch. According to Aswynn, the torch symbolizes knowledge. For Wiccans, light symbolizes what we might call a "daytime" knowledge, what our eyes and intellect show us, as distinct from the intuitive, feeling-oriented knowledge of darkness.

In *Teutonic Magic: The Magical and Spiritual Practices of the Germanic People*, author Kveldulf Gundarsson suggests a different interpretation of the torch, relating it to Cen's other meaning, "swelling." He bases his understanding on ancient burial practices: The earliest custom was to bury a body until the flesh rotted off the bones, at which point, he says, the flesh may have been used in burial rites (later, cremation became customary). Both meanings of Cen (Kenaz in the Elder Futhark) had to do with the disposal of dead bodies, and with the wisdom ascribed to the dead.

How does this relate to Wicca's association of the Autumn Equinox with harvest? Well, of course, to harvest a plant or an animal is to kill it. Nowadays, we tend to think of harvest in terms of gain, of abundance and survival, but the truth is that life feeds on life, and our lives are sustained by the death of that which we eat. Our knowledge that we will survive the fallow Winter months is based on the success of the hunt and the harvest, on the death of game and crops. And just as one focus of the Asatru faith is on our obligation to our ancestors, those on whose lives ours are built, one of Wicca's focuses is on the God's willing death in hunt and harvest, which sustains our bodies, and on the wisdom of the cycle of death and rebirth, which sustains our spirits.

The Runic cognate for the English alphabet's letter *R* traditionally means, according to both Freya Aswynn and Kveldulf Gundarsson, "riding." Alternate and related meanings include "wagon" and "journey." But Aswynn points out that this Rune (called Raido in the Elder Futhark) is called Rad in Anglo-Saxon, and the word *rad* is related to the German and Dutch words for "counsel." Aswynn believes it's also related to another Gothic word, *raiht*, which translates in English as both "doing the right thing" and "dispensing judgment."

Whether or not her etymology is correct, those ideas give us a lot to think about. How can we relate those meanings—"riding," "wagon," "journey," "counsel," "doing the right thing," and "dispensing judgment"—to Wicca's Sabbat of Mabon?

"Wagon" is the easiest: Think of the wagons on which harvest bounty is taken to market! Taking bales of wheat, baskets of apples, bags of potatoes, and loads of other vegetables to market is a journey. But the process of harvest itself can be considered a journey, too, both literally as a harvester works through the rows in the field, and spiritually as we consider the social and emotional consequences of our behavior and decisions throughout the year. The harvest "rides" to the market, and we "ride" the emotional tides of our lives, of our joy in successful harvests, and our worry if there doesn't seem to be enough to keep us through the Winter.

Freya Aswynn writes in *Leaves of Yggdrasil* that this Rune "relates to the ability to move within one's natural limits, and consequently to become aware of what these limits are." She suggests that working with this Rune "means to be in charge of your own path in life; to keep your own counsel; to ride, not to be ridden...." These are certainly fitting interpretations for Wiccans. Doing the right thing is something we always hope to achieve, but "right" doesn't apply exclusively to moral decisions. In terms of bringing literal or figurative crops to bear, we always have to make some guesses, based on our experience, our intellectual knowledge (guided by Cen or Kenaz, the torch), and our intuition, and we don't always guess right. Whether we've done the right thing or not, and how much we are in charge of our own life, can't always be determined on the basis of a single event. It often takes whole seasons to see a final outcome, just as it takes whole seasons to bring a crop to maturity.

Kveldulf Gundarsson tells us that Rad (Raido) is "above all, a rune of ordered movement—movement in space, movement in time, and the relationship between the two." Extending that definition means that the journey Rad refers to is our journey through life itself, through the cycle of birth, growth, death, and rebirth. Clearly, then, it's an appropriate Rune to consider at Mabon, when harvest focuses us on the death that serves life both by sustaining us through the Winter and ensuring rebirth in the Spring.

Gifu (Gebo in the Elder Futhark) means "gift." Its meaning doesn't lie in the modern context of a prettily wrapped birthday present, though. The concept here is much wider, having to do with a quality of leadership, of generosity, of hospitality. In fact, the ideas behind this Rune are common to both the Anglo-Saxon (and the Northern) and the Celtic cultures, from which Wicca is derived. The Rune looks like an intersection at which two distinct paths cross. It is an intersection of the Anglo-Saxon (and the Northern) and the Celtic cultures at the point of hospitality and, chiefly, generosity—values these cultures share. This Rune thus represents a very special gift for Wiccans: the gift of common heritage from these two sources.

Aswynn discusses several extended meanings of Gifu: "balance," "reciprocation," and even "betrothal"! Gundarsson brings up the Rune's representation of alliances sealed, and the Rune's relationship to the world's gift to Odin and Odin's gift to the world of Runes themselves. This Rune, Gundarsson says, "governs both the religious work of sacrificing to the Gods and the mystical work of sacrificing self to self...."

It's worth pointing out again that Wicca doesn't sacrifice the ways ancient Pagans did with literal lifeblood; we offer our efforts and accomplishments, our commitments, our joys and sorrows, and our dreams and fears, in thanks and for transformation, to the Gods. That said, we can also say that all the nuances of gifting included in the significance of Gifu apply very well to the Wiccan celebration of Mabon.

Our God leads us...through the gates of death and back again to renewed life In leading us, He not only gifts us with various aspects of His life, but receives from us gifts of our energies. In one sense, it is this very relationship that constitutes the abundance of our harvests. Our God hospitably shares His perfect love and perfect trust with us, shares His knowledge of the way from death to rebirth, and shares the abundance of His energy in the harvests that keep us alive. We offer Him our faith in return. We offer each other the hospitality of our tables, and the hospitality of our hearts as well.

Though it's not among any of the meanings I've read for Gifu (Gebo), I can't help noticing that its form might be taken as a glyph for not only the intersections of Wicca's parent cultures, but for the sheaves of corn and wheat that often symbolize Mabon. For all these reasons, I think that Gifu is the most significant to Wiccans of the Runes that can be associated with the Autumn Equinox, which we celebrate as Mabon.

Mabon Recipes

"John Barleycorn" is an old harvest song. Ostensibly, it's about a fellow named John Barleycorn who is set upon by three men from the West, who murder him. But as the verses carry on, we hear that the men leave him for dead in a field, and are amazed (as is everyone else) when John Barleycorn rises up again in the Spring. They're amazed all Summer long, and come Autumn, they kill him again, grinding and fermenting his body. Yet, "he lived to tell the tale, for they poured him out of an old brown jug, and they call him home-brewed ale."

We all know that John Barleycorn lives on in more than ale. He's with us every year in home-baked bread as well. To further honor him—or rather "Him," for the name is one of the God's—here's a recipe for a barley soup.

Mushroom and Barley Soup

You will need 6 cups of vegetable stock, at least 1 1/4 cups of chopped onion, 2 cloves of garlic (minced), 4 tablespoons of dry sherry, 4 tablespoons of soy sauce (more or less, to taste), 2 teaspoons of dry dill, 1 cup of medium pearl barley, and 1 pound of fresh mushrooms (sliced).

Once you've rinsed and drained the barley, cover it in 1 1/2 cups of the vegetable stock, and cook until tender. Meanwhile, in a separate pan, sauté the onions and garlic until they are translucent (use olive oil or cooking spray for this). When the onions and garlic are translucent, come out of the trance the divine smell has induced, and add the mushrooms and the sherry. Cook everything, uncovered, until the mushrooms are soft.

Finally, add the mushroom mixture to the barley, along with the rest of the stock and the remaining ingredients. Bring the soup to a boil, uncovered, and then reduce the heat. Cover the pot and leave it to simmer for about 20 minutes. It is now ready to be served! You might like a bit of bread with this—anything from sourdough to a hearty rye, depending on your taste. You might also like a glass of ale with this soup. Whatever you're drinking, don't forget to toast John Barleycorn!

Squash

Squash is nutritious, delicious, and good to serve at Mabon. There are plenty of squash recipes available, but some of us (I'm waving my hand from the keyboard here) are not, shall we say, recipe-oriented. For people like me, squash is really ideal because it's just plain easy!

Zucchini is a squash with which most of us are familiar, and one of the simplest to prepare. Wash it, peel it (there are nutrients in the skin, just like there are in the skins of most fruits and vegetables, so you might want to leave it on), and slice it. Next, steam it until it is tender. Put a little butter (or butter substitute) on it, salt and pepper to taste, and there you are!

Most other squashes are equally cooperative, although some require seeding or other "degutting" before you can use them. But slicing or chopping them into bite-size pieces and then steaming or baking them until they are tender gets them ready for you to eat. If you're baking your squash, remember to spray the pan with one of those nonstick cooking sprays. Apart from that, there's nothing to it!

ymbols

Before we look at some of Mabon's symbols, let's take another look at the Wheel as a whole. Mabon is the Autumn Equinox. On American calendars, the Autumn Equinox is noted as the beginning of Autumn, but on Wicca's Wheel of the Year, it is mid-Autumn. For Wiccans, Autumn begins at Lammas and ends at Samhain, when Winter begins.

Why if Autumn begins at Lammas and Mabon is mid-Autumn, are both of these holidays included in a book about the Summer Sabbats? It's because in the old days, the Year was divided into two seasons: Summer and Winter. Summer began (and by Wiccan reckoning still begins) at Beltane. Winter began (and on Wicca's calendar still begins) at Samhain. When you draw a line across the Wheel from Samhain to Beltane, you see that Samhain, Yule, Imbolc, and Ostara constitute one season (Winter), and Beltane, Litha, Lammas, and Mabon constitute the other (Summer).

Over time, the agricultural and astronomical calendars have been combined, and now we recognize four seasons in the Year. We still honor the original division, though, so Winter includes Spring, and Summer includes Autumn. And because Mabon is an Equinox, a time of balance and transition, Mabon shares some of Autumn's symbols with Lammas and Samhain, the Sabbats that surround it.

Acorns

Acorns are at the top of our list of Mabon symbols, and not just because they start with the letter *A*. As perfectly as eggs symbolize Ostara, acorns represent Mabon. They're the "fruit" of the oak, and so part of the harvest. They're also the seed, and so the promise of rebirth. Like every fruit, they represent the death of a flower, and, as we've seen, flowers are vibrant symbols of vigorous life. And like every fruit, acorns contain the seed of the next generation, fulfilling the Goddess's promise and the God's destiny of rebirth.

Antlers and Horns

One of Wicca's most popular chants, which we begin to sing at Lammas and Mabon, is "Hoof and Horn." "Hoof and horn," it goes, "hoof and horn; all that dies shall be reborn." Both horns and antlers are phallic, which is fairly obvious in their early stages of growth. The phallus itself dies and is reborn rather often, but this is a symbol we can't confine to one particular Sabbat!

Horns, of course, grow on an animal's head for life, lengthening as the seasons turn and reflecting in their sharpness or bluntness an animal's successes and defeats. Taken from the dead, they're fashioned into drinking vessels. They are also made to sound as signals to begin or end hunts or other community events, or to call for support or succor. At Mabon, we do all of these things: We sound our horns, one way or another, to signal life's persistence through death, to signal that death occurs in the service of life.

Antlers' symbolism is even more obvious. We do make a few things from antlers or tines of antlers—knife, rattle, and utensil handles mostly. But the significant thing about them is that the animals who bear them shed them every Autumn. They are a male beast's crown through the Summer, displaying his strength, vigor, and worthiness. Yet, when the rut is over, when he has proved his points, we might say, he drops them. He grows them anew next year, demonstrating that we're not "reborn" only through our offspring. Life responds individually and as a whole to death and rebirth in many ways. Dropping and regrowing antlers is the stag's way of refocusing his energies as the seasons roll past.

Most of us consider it propitious to find antlers in the woods. Hunters usually keep the antlers of the bucks they kill, and the more tines or "points" the antlers have, the worthier the beast, and the stronger, more formidable challenger. Canyondancer and I don't hunt, but we have a modest set of antlers from my dad's bow-hunting days, and we occasionally give it a place of honor in ritual. Friends and family have gifted us with small segments of antler over the years, and we respect them all as representative of our God.

By the way, the horns you see on stereotypical Viking helmets are just that—stereotypical. Probably there were horns on some ceremonial helmets (that's true of most cultures), but their battle helmets were unadorned. Just imagine close combat while wearing a horned helmet, and imagine the ways you could become entangled, indefensibly restrained, while your neck is snapped by an enemy.

But the Vikings did, and the Asatru do today, sound magnificent ceremonial hunting horns (yes, like the ones in the *The Lord of the Rings* movies) and raise toasts in drinking horns. Some of these are elaborately carved, and some used by the Valkyries (ritual Priestesses) are enormous. Some Druids and Wiccans carry drinking horns too. And, of course, many Wiccan Priests wear antlered headdresses.

Cornucopias

The cornucopia is another symbol of Mabon. As we've already discussed, some Wiccans liken Mabon to the American holiday of Thanksgiving, for which the cornucopia is also a well-understood symbol. In many cultures, goddesses of plenty (associated with Summer, as well as with Autumn) carry cornucopias. Because they're filled with harvest fruits and vegetables, it's easy to see cornucopias as harvest baskets.

Once we're reminded, it's also easy to see the cornucopia itself as a sort of horn-shaped cauldron, a symbol of the Goddess's womb. Of course, the fruits and grains within it are symbols of the God, the God of the Grain, the God of the Vine: the son of the Goddess, the fruit of Her womb. Containing as it does the harvest and the seed, the cornucopia is a mundane-looking representation of the God's death, the Goddess's loss, and the promise of rebirth. The grains, fruits, and vegetables we see overflowing the cornucopia symbolize life overflowing the grave-become-womb.

The harvest sustains us in more ways than one: Through the Winter we survive on the flesh of the fruit and grain, and through the years we survive by participating in the cycle of death and rebirth. The cornucopia, if we think about it, symbolizes the transformation that is the turning of the Wheel, the constant transformation, season after season, that we celebrate.

Dry Leaves

Dry leaves symbolize Mabon too. Straightforwardly, they're what we see every Autumn, and they are tangible tokens of the physical process that trees go through in their own celebration of the seasons of life.

Sometimes it makes me smile and shake my head to see how many of us are willing to appreciate the beauty of dried leaves—you can find wreaths of them for sale in catalogs and craft shops—and how few of us are able to appreciate death in other forms. When we see leaves fallen from trees, we naturally think ahead to the buds that will burst forth again next Spring. It's harder for most people to remember that rebirth follows all death in just the same way, but that's exactly what dry leaves "mean" to Wiccans.

Many dried leaves fade to brown, but in a lot of them you can see traces of red and gold, the colors of flame, the colors of the spark of life that remains in trees that have dropped their leaves. The bright Autumn leaves we all love (whether for their color or their crunch underfoot) remind us that life does indeed follow death. Even when the color has faded from Autumn leaves and we can crunch them underfoot, they're part of the life cycle. They mulch the new trees that are gestating in their seeds, getting ready to sprout next year.

In layers on the park or forest floor, dry leaves provide shelter for wee burrowing beasties and sustenance for insects. Before they nourish the streambed, the algae, and the more sophisticated plants that grow there and in ponds, they provide haven for fish, sheltering them from predators' view. Old clumps of leaves that collect on the banks and against logs fallen across a stream keep the water cool in the Summer too, helping to preserve habitat and resources for wildlife...and for wild children who are lucky enough to enjoy streams and swimmin' holes!

Gourds

Gourds, like dry leaves, are gorgeous, and we often use them for decoration. First, of course, they are food: Squash is one of the four staple foods of the world (along with corn, wheat, and rice). Most squashes are at least vaguely womb-shaped, and those that aren't take the shape of the womb's complement, the phallus. Indeed, as any seed-bearing food is, gourds are symbols of the Goddess and God's relationship, and of the cycle of life, death, and rebirth. Like leaves, their bright colors remind us of the spark of life that is in all things, no matter what step they're taking in the Spiral Dance. And don't forget that once they're dried, gourds can become rattles, too, and help us keep the rhythm of the Dance!

Grapes

Grapes are very popular symbols of Mabon. In bunches and even as jelly, grapes are part of many feasts. In these forms they represent the flesh of the God, whose many aspects feed us. They also take the form of wine, which symbolizes life's blood. When we eat of the grape or drink of the wine, we're not just tasting His body and His blood (although, in some religions the focus is concentrated on this symbolism). Wicca understands that all plants are forms of the foliate aspect of the God, sacred and holy in themselves, not just heraldic symbols of deity. Therefore, the symbolism of grapes for Wiccans is even wider.

The image of the Green Man, the God's foliate form, is often drawn so that some of the greenery takes the shape of horns, because, in any aspect of the God, we can see all the aspects of the God. In the same way, grapes symbolize all the fruits, vegetables, and grains that we recognize as the body of the God of the Grain. Because they're so fleshy and ripen in Autumn, grapes can also represent all the animals we recognize as the body of the God of the Game. We've bred seedless grapes now (what's up with *that*?), but "real" grapes have seeds, as all life forms do one way or another, so that in them exists both the life of the generation that feeds on them and the life of the generation that will spring from them. Responding to their environments, grapes even come in several colors and varieties, and so even more deeply represent the diversity of life and the cooperative ways in which life feeds on life.

But wait, there's more! Grapes make wine! As grapes grow on the vine, they're very earthy; as wine, they encompass all of water's symbolism: amniotic fluid that nourishes in the womb, "juice" that nourishes our bodies, and "water" that cleans us. No, you can't take a bath in wine and come out looking clean, but red wine is said to help keep our arteries clear, and that is also an important kind of cleansing! Wine serves every culture's communion, for in some ways it changes our perception, it can transport us to the Otherworld, or at least bring us to the Gates. This makes the source of wine, grapes, a particularly significant symbol of Mabon, a time when we are balanced between light and darkness.

Rattles

We've already noticed that rattles can be made from gourds. Dried seeds, and sometimes small stones, crystals, or small bits of broken things, turn gourds and other hollow containers into noisemakers. The noise they make is the noise of life. The rattle's sound is a cousin to the rustle of corn husks, the whisper of a growing field, the footsteps of wild beasts that symbolize other aspects of the Wiccan God. The rattle's sound is an echo of the surf's lullabies, of a brook's babbling, of feet stirring up dust as they dance. The rattles' staccato sounds remind us of drums, of the falling of an axe upon a log, of grunts that accompany the efforts of life and death. The time we can keep with rattles is the regular time of our heartbeats, multiplied by those of the lives that surround us, and the irregular rhythms of memory and dream. At Mabon we are balanced, but leaning toward Winter, and our rattles remind us of both the world's busy Summer activities and the trance-like introspective work of Winter.

onclusion

The WordPerfect page fills my screen, the same way fresh sheets of paper used to stand up from my old typewriters' rollers, and as I consider how to close this volume of *Celebrating the Seasons of Life*, the January sky is blue outside my window. Mind you, it's cold out there, and the luminarias that decorate the roof for the holidays are still up. (As I revise my manuscript, it's February's blue skies I see, but we still haven't taken the luminarias down.) It's a funny time to be writing about Summer Sabbats. On the other hand, the perspective we have on Summer now, not long after Yule, is certainly an appreciative one.

Beltane has always been my favorite Sabbat. I love the fairy magic associated with it, and I love how my Tradition and my coven celebrate it. We've been lucky enough to realize our ideal more than once by bringing our fairy-tale visions to life in the warm woods of Southeastern Arizona's National Forests. Even when I know that it won't be like that every year, and maybe even never again, the memories of "perfect" Beltane celebrations bring joy to my anticipation of future rites, and joy to the rites themselves.

That's what's supposed to happen, of course. As we celebrate each Sabbat and each season of life, we're supposed to fondly remember the one just past, while glancing forward toward the Wheel's next turning. Just as we are literally warmed by the Summer Sun, we're supposed to be figuratively warmed by our knowledge that the Wheel does keep turning, from season to season.

We're supposed to feel core-warmed by each season's likeness to its last-year self, and we're supposed to be mystery-sparked by each season's undeniable individuality. There are times, of course, when we're oblivious to wonder, but that's what Sabbats are for—to reconnect us, through celebration of the seasons, with the wonder of life.

Beltane and Mabon

At first glance, Beltane and Mabon look quite different. Beltane is all ribbons and fairy dust, sunshine and dancing steps (if you're old enough, whether you're Pagan or not, you'll remember Jethro Tull's evocative song, "Velvet Green"). Mabon is when Beltane's budding leaves turn color and fall from their trees, when blooms fade and shed their seeds, when animals begin to fatten themselves up and dig in or head south. Mabon is when, in most places, your sweaters and coats see the diminishing light of day after weeks in the bottom of a drawer or the back of a closet. Beltane twirls the world with glee; Mabon pulls it in again toward a guarded hearth.

The God at Beltane is carefree and lusty. Most of us picture Him as the Green Man or Pan, ready to enliven the worlds, if not yet mature enough to rule them wisely. By Mabon, He is dead or dying, having entrusted all His energies to us. At Beltane, our May dances, whatever form they take, pledge us to grow with Him, to share our creativity with the worlds as the God and Goddess share Their fertilities. At Mabon, we pledge ourselves to Them again, but differently now, promising to husband Their gifts, apportioning them for the honor of the past, the security of the present, and the endowment of the future.

The Summer Sabbats, bracketed by Beltane and Mabon, are the life cycle *in action*. By some Traditions' reckoning, the Summer months belong to the God, for not only is His symbol, the Sun strongest then, but Summertime is when most of us are most active. Broadly, the God represents projection and activity, complemented by the Goddess's receptivity and stillness. Summer is when cells are *in action*. It is over the Summer that kids amaze us with their growth spurts, and when we hope to see fields, gardens, and herds growing too.

There is more to a Year than Beltane, Litha, Lammas, and Mabon, of course, just as there is more to a baby than the months between birth and the first birthday. We cherish the Winter Sabbats as much as we do pregnancy, and, indeed, both may bring forth our sense of wonder even more than what follows. But a bouncing baby engages us more actively, and the Summer Sabbats give us an opportunity to experience our physical lives as sacred. This experience is too uncommon in our recent cultural experience.

It's not that our culture doesn't focus on our physical attributes. If, on a given day, you counted the number of articles and books about bodies, from perspectives ranging from crassly carnal to concern for the psychological trauma our children experience when their humanity is confused with the shape of their bodies and the color of their skin, your count would be outdated by day's end. If you tried to count the pictures, you'd have to learn new numbers. Our culture can't seem to integrate its perception of our physical forms.

There's the image of tanned beauty, but never mind that few men and women really look like that, and never mind that tanning is to cancer what opening a window is to a storybook vampire. There is the image of the wanton slut, and never mind that women in sweat suits have been said to be "asking for" rape, and never mind that the most advertised and most prominently displayed clothes are the ones that we condemn women for wearing. There's the image of the devoted mother, and the notion that breasts are purely prurient. There's the principle that sex sells, and the premise that sex is wicked.

But at the Summer Sabbats, we can take ourselves outside for a healthy dose of sunshine and enjoy the ritual proclamation that our bodies are the bodies of the Gods. In the field trips or vacations we may take with our coveners or with non-Pagan friends, we have a chance to appreciate each other's good sportsmanship and skills without needing to compare each other to magazine models. Field stains and scrapes aside, a softball dived for and safely caught, a volleyball well-returned for the team, or a friend's well-wielded net when we've got a big ol' trout on the line can be an equivalent in our lives to Lugh's long-armed spear throwing or battle victories. Summer Sabbats and feasts, and the sparkling eyes and unselfconscious laughter they generate, are proof for us that our bodies are sacred.

When we look across the Wheel from Beltane, we see Samhain. Much of the prejudice against Wicca that remains in our society is centered on Samhain, which is wildly misinterpreted every year. Ironically, many of those who accuse Samhain of Satanic tendencies remember dancing the Maypole in their schoolyards. The idea that spirit and flesh are opponents, and that flesh succors "evil" while spirit shelters "good," is most often and most clearly expressed in criticisms of Samhain and the horrifying rituals ascribed to it. Beltane, miraculously, remains unsullied by the fear and ignorance that has vilified Samhain. And, if we can't save our ghosts from fundamentalist demonization, we can still rejoice that our Maypoles haven't been illegal since the late 18th century.

At Beltane, it's warm enough just about everywhere to make the holiest of sacraments outside. Yes, that's right: It is at Beltane that the Great Rite is most often performed in the bodies of a Priestess and Priest, rather than with the cup and the athame. Mind you, this isn't the case in every Circle; the *hieros gamos*, the sacred marriage, is sacred in that "token" form too. I've never met a Pagan, though, Wiccan, Asatru, or Druid, who hasn't made or enjoyed at least a joke about dancing the Maypole in private parts...of the wood. At Beltane, more than any other time, we dare to admit that, yes, the body is sacred and sex is a fitting offering to the Gods.

At Mabon, the other offering of flesh is made. At Mabon, bodies rejoice in death rather than in copulation. But, in a way, death is a form of copulation. At Beltane, individuals mate on the physical plane; at Mabon, Individuality conjoins with, "mates" with, Wholeness. Just as incarnate fertility is assured and celebrated at Beltane, so our connection with the spirit world is reaffirmed at Mabon. (Taking the longer perspective this book has stayed aware of, this reunion of matter and spirit began at Lammas and comes to its climax, as it were, at Samhain.) One of the aspects of balance that Mabon, the Autumn Equinox, is about is the balance between the worlds of spirit (as in soul and psyche) and matter, which Wicca holds equally real, relevant, and sacred.

Beltane is not an Equinox, and by then, in the Northern Hemisphere, the balance of the Year has tilted decisively toward Summer, but Beltane speaks to the marriage of spirit and matter in another way. Beltane is a fairy Sabbat, and the wedding of the Goddess and the God that occurs at Beltane is another re/union of the spirit world—spirits as in fairies—and the matter men and woman are made of. These realms, too, magical and mundane, Wicca also holds equally real, relevant, and sacred.

Wheel Tracks

In the Conclusion of the first book of this set, I said, "No book, no matter how in-depth its research, no matter how comprehensive its range, can say everything there is to say about any Sabbat." This is true, I said, because "every season we celebrate adds more to the experience of life," and all our research and all our explanations add to what there is for us to understand. As long as it has been since you read the first of these books, or as long as it will be until you do, that will still be true. And the more you pay attention to the seasons of your own life, the more you'll know it.

"The more things change, the more things stay the same." Have you heard that before? Sure you have. I think that turning it around makes it even more true from Wicca's perspective: "the more things stay the same, the more they change." This is certainly true in the way Wicca celebrates the seasons of life. Even when we conduct our Sabbats with the same script every year, whether we read it or memorize it, even when we meet in the same place at the same time and bring to our feasts the same foods, we are not reliving old moments, we are living new ones.

Recently, a good friend's father died. My parents and her mother predeceased him, and now both my family's home and her family's home have been sold. When she sent pictures of her folks' house, empty and ready for its new family's furniture, a strange feeling came over me. I recognized in it the touch of Wyrd, which is sometimes translated from the Anglo-Saxon as "fate," but which is more than that. This was my friend's family's house, but I have my own memories of it, and even in the few pictures she sent, I could see that some of my memories are changed from what my experience must have been. Was there really a door *there*? Was there a *step* there? The rose bush was *that* close to the street?

I assume my memories of my family's house have undergone similar changes. Do these changes make my memories wrong? Well, from an architect's point of view, yeah. But are they untruthful, really? I think not. Because it's not the houses or the yards I'm remembering; it's what happened there and the events through which my relationships, with her and with our families, unfolded. The houses and yards were, in my experience, like theatrical sets for those relationships and for our growth in those relationships. In my memory, walls and stairs and even rosebushes move to accommodate my growing understanding of those relationships.

When, in those pictures—the ones I've taken of our coven's activities through the years, the ones I'll take of our daughter coven's activities, the ones I take at T.A.W.N.'s Fall festival—I see what changes my memory has wrought, I may find the differences bittersweet, but even so, I cherish the recognition of change. It's as precious as those marks we make to measure our children's heights as they stand in their stockinged feet against our doorjambs. Growth is what we're here for, and old pictures, whatever other feelings they rouse in me, offer me proof that we're doing what we came for. Good for us! Huzzah!

Even though everything does change from year to year, sometimes we prefer to suspend our disbelief and enjoy the thought that some things don't. This is a true thought in at least one way: the past is always there, and even when our memories revise it, we're usually unaware of it unless we have the photo album in our laps.

Our perception and appreciation of change tends to be selective. When change means we can go to the potty and get dressed by ourselves, or that we can finally take the car out on our own, we welcome it. When it's about seeing the kids off to college, needing reading glasses, or accepting that the value of our retirement funds has plummeted, we might find it less auspicious. However we feel about change, though (and however we acknowledge it or don't), it's fundamental to our lives.

Everyone has been glad to see a horrible day end so that a better one can dawn, or glad to wake up on the morning that starts a vacation. That sunrise will follow the dark hours of night is a constant change, and one we rely upon. We rely upon seasons changing, too, and let's not forget that, as Wiccans, the magic we do is intended to effect change in the world.

Did you know that natural rates of exfoliation replace your skin completely once a month? At different rates, according to Dr. Deepak Chopra in *Ageless Body, Timeless Mind*, every organ in your body is changed—renewed—several times in your life; your stomach lining is reformed more than 70 times in a single year! If you're Wiccan, you believe in reincarnation, which is another cycle of change. Like a Beltane Maypole dance, and like the swirling gusts that whirl Autumn's falling leaves at our feet, the seasons—and we with them—go round and round the Wheel, celebrating at every turn.

Appendix A
Living-Room Wicca

Yes, Wicca is a "Nature Religion." What this means (among other things) is that instead of relying on written scripture, we look to the natural world(s) to see what's right and holy. It is wonderful, inspiring, and impressive when we can practice our Nature Religion *in Nature*, but the truth is that for myriad reasons, not all of us can, or want to, go outside for the Sabbats and Moons.

Quite a lot of Wiccans never cast a Circle out of doors, and a goodly number never have the chance to participate in an outdoor Circle. I do think that's too bad, but I don't hold it against anyone, even if it is entirely by choice that they're a mostly or exclusively indoor practitioner. I am pleased to be able to celebrate several Sabbats a year in the woo-ids, and to salute the Moon from the Circle in my yard, but I recognize that many of my brothers and sisters in the Craft work inside most, if not all, of the time.

I respect them and their reality. Although I'm willing to brave some wind and rain, various slopes and terrains, along with 100° F (37° C)—or higher—temperatures and darksome nights, I frankly prefer to see snow on Yule cards or through windows. And as Nature's example is that our diversity gives us strength, I appreciate that other people have different preferences. My work as a spiritual counselor to Wiccans in prison reminds me that one of my responsibilities is to stop whining and find a way.

That's why I am going to talk about working inside. Maybe you're not casting your Circle in a living room. Maybe you are using your bedroom, a garage, or the dining-room table. Maybe you're confined to a bathroom or a basement. This doesn't matter. You already know that "better it would be" if you could be outside under the Sun or stars, but for reasons of your own (by choice or by constraint; indefinitely or temporarily), you're inside. There's no need for you to feel inferior or chastised about this, but if you're a beginner or new to working indoors, there may well be a need for some ideas about transforming your everyday spaces into temples.

Maybe you're not sure how to cast a Circle. In Appendix A of this book's sister volume (*Celebrating the Seasons of Life: Samhain to Ostara*) you'll find detailed instructions, complete with all the "magic words" you'll need. I suggest that if you don't have your own "usual way" of casting, you get a copy of that book. But for quick reference right now, there is an Order of Circle in the box beside this paragraph.

Now, before we look at some ways that you can keep the "Nature Religion" flavor of Wicca while you're working inside, I want to talk a little more about the whys and wherefores of living-room worship. The first thing to understand is that a lot of religions are actually meant to be practiced indoors. In many cases, that's because their fundamental understanding of the world is that there's a separation between Nature and Civilization.

Order of Circle

1. Prepare your salt and water.
2. Cast the Circle with Fire.
3. Bless the Circle with Salt and Water.
4. Charge the Circle with Air.
5. Call the Quarters.
6. Invoke the Goddess and God.
7. Work your magics *or* enact your Sabbat rites.
8. Celebrate Cakes and Ale (Note: Some Traditions celebrate Cakes and Ale before they work magic or enact Sabbat rites).
9. Thank the Gods.
10. Dismiss the Quarters.
11. Undraw the Circle (if necessary).

The walls of our buildings keep the nasty old natural world outside, and us safely inside, away from diurnal and seasonal changes in temperature, away from temptations and dangers.

Being fair, indoor spaces make it easier to gather in inclement weather, facilitate a proximity that can encourage community, and often have better acoustics than outdoor venues. But, historically, there have been other considerations. If the natural world is base, carnal, and uncontrollable, indoor spaces are lofty (which is why most churches have high ceilings) and spiritual: Not only are they neat and clean, but they are made of expensive materials that are usually uncommon to that specific area. Co-incidentally (or maybe not), the people in them can be monitored and controlled, made to move and speak in unison, and made subject to sanctions for worshiping outside the lines.

Wicca actually developed from a rejection of this way of thinking. The Inquisition wasn't really about lingering Paganism, it was about heresy, about suppressing people's natural (there's that word again!) inclination to figure out for themselves what holy men and phenomena mean, and to have, well, religious experiences without anyone else's help. Not only was European Paganism pretty well gone by the time the Inquisition got started, but Paganism had mostly been of the state religion variety, and just as oppressive, in its own way, as monotheism became when there was just the one Church.

Even though the old forms of Paganism were autocratic and restrictive, too, they did offer one thing that was missing from monotheistic theologies: goddesses. Oh, sure, there were "feminine principles" involved in early Christianity, but they were sidekicks, broadly speaking, to the more powerful male principles. Mary, you'll recall, was eventually accorded Mother of God status, but it still wasn't (and isn't) permitted to worship her in her own right.

Well, okay, but people still depended on what we might call Goddess-functions to survive. Fertility, domestic maintenance, and the health of people, herds, and resources such as rivers and wells had all been under the care of goddesses, and for our Western European ancestors, putting masculine deities in charge was not a wholly good thing. The oppression of women, exhaustion and pollution of natural resources, and power-over complexes running rampant were among the results. People wanted their Mommy, but calling out for Her put them in serious peril. Most of Her names went unspoken for so long that people forgot what they wanted, but they couldn't shake the vague feeling that *something* was missing.

This isn't a history book, but it's helpful to realize that it was during the Middle Ages that the natural world, women, and evil came to be part of the same gestalt. Resisting the Inquisition, Martin Luther's Protestantism deflected some of the Church's flak, and, late in the Renaissance, poets and other authors started to assail the "Nature is horrible" construct. The 18th century's Industrial Revolution, with its pollution and its sundering of traditional families, contributed mightily to a reversal of people's perceptions of Nature and Civilization.

Suddenly, *cities* were wild and dangerous while the *countryside* seemed peaceful and safe. Thus was the Romantic Movement born, and it ultimately begat Wicca. In the pastoral fields and the thrillingly dark woods of 18th-century and 19th-century Europe and Britain, the goddesses and gods of old were made over and reintroduced to a public starved for the divine feminine. It's not that all the devout city churchgoers left to romp in the country with Pan and Diana, but it *is* like they weren't quite so easy to intimidate any longer.

Gerald Gardner's Wicca embodies 200 years of poetry, prose, philosophy, art, and science, and a prodigious paradigm shift that is still a beacon as the 21st century begins. It's not just its "feminist" thealogy that distinguishes Wicca, but several other fundamental facets as well. And, wherever we practice our religion, we seek to capture them all.

Most of us know that Wicca's cultural heritage is Anglo-Celtic, and we rightly enjoy searching out stories of the old gods and goddesses, such as Brigid and Lugh, and Cerridwen and Llyr, and influential heroes such as Cuchulain, Arthur, and Robin Hood. But our cultural heritage is broader than that, and includes ideas that are alive and important to us all today.

Wicca's about responsible individuality (a social concept that evolved to its current strength during the centuries that eventually generated modern Witchcraft), about the value of human experience as sacramental. Wicca's about the authority and sanctity of the natural world, and about humanity as a native species rather than a special creation. Wicca's about the dignity and worth we share with the rest of life and our environment, about the interrelatedness of it all. Our passwords apply in a larger context than our covens; "perfect love and perfect trust" pass us through the Gates of the universe, no matter how small the dimension we occupy, no matter how vast we ever discover it to be.

So. When we say that Wicca is a Nature Religion, a religion of experience, and a Goddess religion, we're saying a lot more than those words convey to most people. And when we understand this, when we remind ourselves of the real magnitude and significance of our faith, we can see that *where* we practice is not as important as it can seem if all you read are books about permanent Circles on farmsteads, private backyards, public lands, or at Ren Faire sites. It's generally accepted (and from my own experience, I have to agree) that an outdoor Circle is the ideal. But don't let anybody tell you that an indoor Circle can't be every bit as beautiful and effective.

That established, let's get a little more specific about ways of accommodating a Wiccan Circle in the ordinarily mundane rooms of our homes.

First things first: Can you move your furniture? Not all of us can. My L-shaped living/dining room is so configured that there's pretty much only one place to put everything. We could push our couch back a foot or so to give us more space in front of the fireplace, but if we did that, our kids would have had to go down the hall, across the kitchen, and back through the dining room to get a tissue without breaking the Circle! You may have similar logistical difficulties.

I could, of course, move the box of tissues to solve this problem, but if you have young children who are torn between a desire to join the

A small, round table holds ritual tools and a bottle of mead. Quarter candles are set on stools and on the hearth. The fourth candle (not pictured) is on an armoire. A Book of Shadows *leans against the altar, and Hal the Kitty rests in a comfortable chair, waiting for the ritual to begin.*

grown-ups in ritual and the opportunity to explore the house without quite so much supervision, moving a box of tissues won't help! Your problems may be with orientation to the Directions or the need for discretion. Maybe you face other challenges entirely.

The suggestions I can give you may not touch your dilemma, or it may not be quite the idea you need—but the point of this Appendix isn't to hand out easy answers. My intention is to get you thinking creatively, perhaps even unconventionally, about ways you can bring more reverence and more mirth to your indoor Circles.

Another point that needs making is that when you're working with an *outdoor* Circle, there's a certain amount of work you need to do before you can conduct your rite. Leaves, possibly fruits, and other detritus need to be cleaned up, grass may need to be mowed, and lawn furniture may need to be moved. Maybe something has to be done about privacy. That necessary work, whatever it is, is an offering to the Gods you'll later invoke into your Circle, and the work itself, as much as where you're doing it, honors your religion and your gods. Equivalent work, and sometimes even more work, must be done to prepare indoor spaces for ritual, and that's true even if you've got a room dedicated to it. Remember that the effort you put into making your indoors ready for ritual is just as well-received by the Gods as any work you do to prepare an outdoor site.

As for exactly how you organize your indoor Circles to maximize both mirth and reverence, lots of things will make a difference. If you have a room you can dedicate to your Circle, one that you never or rarely have to use for any other purpose, then you probably don't have many excuses for not expressing your Traditional or eclectic preferences pretty strongly. If you're a homeowner, you can:

- ✹ Use paintable caulk or joint compound in the creation of dimensional murals on your walls, painting Elemental scenes or symbols.

- ✹ Build niches into your walls for your Quarter candles or for deity images.

- ✹ Construct a permanent stage or altar area.

- ✹ Install wooden or concrete decorative pillars.

- ✹ Use stain or paint to create intricate parquetry or mosaic designs on the floor.

✣ Paint a night and/or day sky on your ceiling.

Even if you rent, you can:

✣ Fasten fabric panels to the walls or cover them with posterboard panels on which you've drawn appropriate Elemental scenes or images of deity.

✣ Create dimensional effects in your room with decorated display boards.

✣ Use an assortment of party supplies (such as colored foil fringe made to cover doorways) to give each Element a home in your "temple room."

Furthermore, some of these adaptations can be ascribed to other interests, such as amateur theater, trying out a decorating idea for a party and liking it well enough to leave up, etc., in the event that Someone Who Mustn't Know You're Wiccan stumbles into the room. Then again, if you have a room you can devote wholly to religious use, you probably don't need me to give you ideas about how to prepare the space—you probably have a million ideas of your own!

It's when you have to use your living room, your dining room, your bedroom, or some other public or semipublic room of your home that you will need ideas. Will it surprise you if I suggest watching some of the popular home-decorating shows on television? Of course, the projects they undertake and the ideas they share aren't overtly Wiccan, but many of their projects and ideas can be modified to meet a Neo-Pagan need. And thinking about ways to adapt their projects to your space can sometimes inspire completely new ideas. It's also true that these shows strongly encourage people to experiment and put such an emphasis on the simplicity of "just repainting" if an idea doesn't work out that if somebody asks about something you don't want to explain, you can always just shrug and say you've been watching too many home decorating shows!

Your budget and time is another critical factor. To be honest, if you can spend a fair amount of money on "stuff," plenty of ideas will probably occur to you. Likewise, if you have lots of time (a whole day to get a room ready for an evening Circle, and another whole day to put everything away again), you probably have lots of ideas you can use.

Maybe you do have a little extra money and a little extra time, and you're just not sure how to use it. If you're a beginner in the Craft, newly solitary, or just forming your own coven and looking to create a distinctive style, you might need some ideas to get you started. As you read these, they'll inspire you with variations and with new ideas of your own—so be ready to jot them down!

First, figure out which way is North. Correctly aligning your Circle to the Directions helps. Once you've got this straight, take a look at what's already at or near the Directions in your room. You can begin your own reorientation, from mundane to sacred, as you vacuum or dust the space you'll be using. But this is only the beginning of your preparation, and I'm not talking about cleaning the bathroom or baking or chilling whatever you're using for Cakes and Ale (or at least I'm not talking only about those things).

Your home holds lots of energy, no doubt pretty good energy overall, that may be distracting to a Circle. You may not need to cleanse the space psychically, in the sense of exorcising it to get rid of bad vibes (and then again, you might!), but you probably at least need to rearrange its energy, much as you might need to rearrange the furniture, to make room for the energies you'll raise in your rites. Here's a spell you can use before you cast a Circle or, with slight modification, anytime the space feels overwhelmed with the exuberance of your mundane life. Cast this spell with your arms stretched wide, turning slowly (deosil) in place. Let spreading your arms out inspire you to a big stretch too—stretching is a wonderful way to ground:

Cleansing the Space Spell

Hear me, walls, and hear me, floor; hear me, ceiling, hear me, space!
What ordinarily you are for is for the moment second place!
Mundane laughter, mundane tears, echoes of mundane concerns,
retreat along with hopes and fear; retreat, upheavals and upturns!
Begone confusion, banished gall; room clear of mem'ry, clear of dream.
Make room for the energy we'll call—be ready here for Circle's gleam!

Once the room has been cleaned by mind as well as by machine, you'll want to continue its transformation to Circle-space. It may seem at first impossible, especially if you've read about and seen pictures of living rooms that look made to order for Wiccan religious meetings. First, remember that everything (and everybody) looks better by candlelight, and, next, read on. The following examples may not meet your every need, but they'll most likely be ideas you can work with:

At my house, the TV used to be at East. We could work with that: For one thing, East is for vision, and the TV is a visual thing, even though it's off during Circles. For another, the digital music channels could provide soft accompaniment to our rites, if we chose to use them. Now, though, our entertainment armoire's been moved, so it's at Southeast, and the 5-foot tall cat post is at East. Except that the cats sometimes crash by us like furry whirlwinds, there's not a particularly significant association there. On the other hand, our cats usually abandon us when we Circle in the living room, so we can put a tray across the top of the cat post and put East's candle there.

There is, conveniently, a fireplace on the south wall of our living room. Even on chilly Winter Moon nights, the body heat of gathered coveners (and the natural extra warmth of a cast Circle) makes a fire uncomfortable, but we can put the Quarter candle there.

If you look out the picture window on the west wall of our house, you can see the fountain that marks West in our outdoor Circle. This fountain could possibly be used to mark West in our indoor Circle, but you can't see it at night because there are no lights shining on it. Along the West edge of our living room there's a chair and a couch, with a table in between. This table is where we place the West Quarter candle. Next to the candle, we could put a bowl of water, a second chalice (the other one is on the altar), a framed picture of the ocean, or my grandmother's conch shell. We could even get one of those tabletop fountains and have melodious moving water at West, or we could drape our hanging lamp with blue cloth or replace the white bulb with a blue one.

Maybe you could move the goldfish bowl to West, or get a goldfish bowl and fill it with shells you've collected on a beach or purchased from a craft store. Maybe you have a pretty bottle (perhaps a blue one) you could fill with seawater. What about a model ship? I'm almost willing to bet that there's something in your home that could symbolize West, and, indeed, other things that could symbolize each of the other Directions too. You might set yourself the quest of finding these objects as part of preparing for your rite.

When we face North from the center of our living-room Circle, we're looking over our couch and into the dining room. Our dining room is too far away to hold the Quarter candle, and the back of the couch, though broad, is rounded (and territory of the cats, who do occasionally venture out to see what we're doing) and not a good place to try balancing a candle.

We've got several options for North. We can move a dining-room chair to the end of the couch, which puts it a little off-center from "actual North," but is still a viable option. We have a small bookcase that we can move behind the couch, and set the Quarter candle on its top shelf. We could also use a serving tray or a dinner plate placed right on the couch to hold North's candle. Other options include attaching a shelf to the wall, on which we could place the Quarter candle, or we could install an unobtrusive plant hook in the ceiling and hang a candle lantern from it. (Remember, using candles indoors is risky, especially around small children and pets, so please keep a fire extinguisher on hand, though it wouldn't be disrespectful to use the Water on the altar in an emergency. Battery candles are acceptable substitutes for flame, and so are flame-shaped light bulbs if you use floor or table lamps at your Quarters.)

We are fortunate to have a small, four-footed round table that we can use for an altar. It doesn't take up too much room in the center of the Circle, and we can orient its feet toward the Directions. The top of the table turns, so we don't have to squeeze by each other to reach it when a Tool one of us needs is on the other side of the altar. It belonged to my mother, and to her mother before her, which seems to me an appropriate lineage for an altar, even if neither Mom nor Grammie were Wiccan. (At the next auspicious time I have free, I plan on refinishing the top, using wood stain to create the appearance of an inlaid pentagram.) Maybe you also have a table you can refinish as an altar, or perhaps you can find one at a thrift shop or garage sale.

Once you have a table (round or square), convert it into an altar with a specially-made cloth. You can buy a ready-made altar cloth from several Pagan stores on the Internet; there might be a local vendor who has something perfect for you. And, of course, you can make your own altar cloth. There are unfinished tables for sale at most home goods stores that are usually not terribly expensive, and you can easily find a solid-colored plain or subtly patterned tablecloth that is wide enough in diameter to cover such a table to the floor. Converting one of these tablecloths into an altar cloth could be easy with fabric paints, or more time-consuming if you want to embroider Quarter symbols on it. You could use it plain if it has to double as a decorative mundane tablecloth.

Any Tools or accessories that you use for mundane purposes as well as in your Circles need to be consecrated, and possibly released from their sacred duties when you're done with your Sabbat or Esbat. This doesn't take much extra work. Here is an all-purpose consecration and release that you can use as is, or modify for use with individual items:

Consecration

Household tools of every day,
of wood and metal, cloth and clay,
by Earth and Fire, by Water and Air,
be now unto magic heir;
and now with holy purpose fill:
so mote it be, as I do will!

Release

By Earth and Water, Air and Fire,
well have you worked to my desire;
so Tools made sacred by decree,
again now ordinary be.
With mundane purpose now refill:
so mote it be, as I do will!

Something else I've heard about what we're calling "living-room Wicca" is that people feel goofy doing all the chants and invocations in such a mundanely familiar place. All I can say about this is, get over it! The truth is, just about everybody feels "goofy" the first few times they speak ritual words aloud. It takes a bit of rehearsal to get the cadence right so rhyming invocations and spells come out sounding both natural and like poetry. It takes a lot of people time to find their "Priest/ess voice" too. (Try a parental voice, or a public speaking voice. No funny accents are necessary, though.)

If your space is lit with candles or one of the alternatives to candles, you'll see less of your familiar furnishings. If you're still distracted by the surroundings, try covering everything with sheets. This will give the room a bit of an abandoned-house feel, and it may make it less familiar so you can get on with your rite. (Be aware that your cats may think you've opened a playground for them, and that this could produce some unusual special effects.)

However, before you go to any great lengths to disguise your room as "not-your-room," consider that there are at least two other ways to get around how goofy you might feel doing Wicca in your living room. One is to just carry on: Recognize that you feel a little silly the first couple of times, and conduct your ritual anyway. You'll get used to it, and it won't take long for it to feel perfectly "natural" to be doing religious rites in there.

The other way is to develop and use your visualization skills. These are skills that you should be working with anyway. They are part of the mental and spiritual discipline that's an important Tool for most Witches. Learning to see your living room as a magician's chamber isn't easy, but it is within your power. Put aside 5 minutes to practice visualization as part of your Circle work. Here's a self-guided meditation you can work with or adapt to meet your needs. This example is to show you what I mean by learning to change the way you see your furniture:

> You've got some piece of furniture to hold your TV and/or stereo. It's not something that you'd expect to see in a temple room...however you think a temple room should look. But it's in the room you need to use as a temple, and you've got to learn to see it as belonging there. So: first think about what, in a "proper" temple room, would be about the size of this piece of furniture of yours. An herb cabinet? A desk where you write out your spells on parchment? A bookcase full of leather-bound tomes of wisdom? The locked cabinet where mysterious spell ingredients are kept away from prying eyes? Once you've settled on what piece of furniture it should be, sit down facing the furniture that exists, and imagine the "proper" furniture in its place. Try to imagine the "right" piece being constructed similarly so that shelves and doors are in roughly the same place. So far, so good—yes?

All right, take it another step. Imagine yourself using the "proper" piece of furniture. See yourself approaching the piece, opening a door, using the quill pen that sits on the shelf, and so forth. Then, open your eyes just a little so that you can physically stand up and move, placing yourself directly in front of the existing furniture. Close your eyes again and, touching a corresponding part of the existing piece, imagine that you're standing before and touching the "proper" furniture. Visualize yourself opening a door and seeing what magical supplies are behind it. Visualize yourself touching it to ground. Take it another step and imagine the scent of the herbs that are stored in the "proper" furniture, the smell of the dragon's blood ink you'd keep on the shelf, etc.

When you use the room magically, avoid looking at the existing furniture directly and with fully open eyes. Let yourself see well enough not to walk into anything, but keep your attention on the lines of the furniture that match the lines of the furniture that "should" be there. Keep some incense handy that mimics the smell of what you'd be keeping on the "proper" shelves. If a quill pen would be visible in your temple room, keep a feather handy and let yourself look at it every now and again. With determination and these few "tricks," you'll soon teach yourself to see the furniture the way you want it to be when you've put space between the Worlds. It's a bit Pavlovian, really, and that's okay. Dogs are guardians in all the Worlds, and your visualization efforts on this plane are creating your temple on the astral.

This brings us to a final caution. If you're doing Wicca in your living room or anywhere else that mundane activities usually take place, you want to be sure that you clear the space of magical energy before it is put to ordinary use again. There are people (and sometimes I'm one of them) who think that it's not always necessary to close a Circle and put its energy away at the end of a ritual, but it's a good habit to develop. It's especially important if you're being private about your religious practices, and if you're still a little self-conscious about casting Circles and conducting or participating in ritual.

Uncasting the Circle is usually adequate; for detailed directions, see Appendix A of *Celebrating the Seasons of Life: Samhain to Ostara*. If you'd like to be really sure the space is returned to its mundane character, try this once you've uncast the Circle and put everything physically back as it was:

Conjuring the Ordinary

By Air and Fire, Water and Earth,
this space has proved its Circle-worth.
I would no magic here detain;
I would return it to mundane.
So go, ye glimmers; begone now, thrill,
and all ye tingles, be now still.
All your glamours, Room, unlearn;
and atmosphere familiar, now return.

ppendix B

What's a Child Ready to Learn About the Summer Sabbats?

As you already know if you have read *Celebrating the Seasons of Life: Samhain to Ostara* (New Page Books, 2004) or *Raising Witches: Teaching the Wiccan Faith to Children* (New Page Books, 2002), I believe that we should make whole-hearted efforts to include our children in the practice of our Neo-Pagan religions. Granted, not every form of celebration is appropriate for children, yet too often children are excluded from Wiccan rites because of groundless prejudice against Wicca itself...or against children.

Lots of people, myself included, have written books about raising children. Some of them focus on how parents should respond to various situations. Of course, you might not feel comfortable with all the proposals, and every parent is bound to face situations such books never mention. What's really helpful is a book that tells you about child development, so you can figure out how to respond to your own kids. As people mature from infancy to adulthood, they have certain needs, they need to learn specific skills, and they need to have particular sorts of experience. It's a parent's job to meet those needs and provide opportunities for their children to learn, and to make those kinds of experiences safe. All this is much easier if parents know something about the way human children normally develop.

Borrowing from "What's a Child Ready to Learn about Wicca?" (a chart from *Raising Witches*), you will find helpful information about introducing your children to the Wiccan religion. This information, covering the five stages of growth for children, is based on several years of research, experience with my own child and my friends' experience with theirs, and on considerable thought about how to raise children in Wicca and other Neo-Pagan religions. It's impossible to share everything I've learned (and, of course, I'm still learning), but one thing I can share is that even though it's important to understand how normal human bodies and minds develop, it's equally, if not more important, to know your own children as individuals—distinct from the "average" and distinct from what we might want them to be.

In the charts that follow, I'm offering guidelines and ideas—not absolutes. Each child's personality and your own inclinations and circumstances will make some suggestions more useful than others. I hope that most of these ideas will work for you, but I also hope to give you an idea of the different ways you can include your children in the practice of our faith.

Don't forget that these suggestions can also apply to your own inner child, and, if you are working with people new to the Craft, student of any age.

Reading these charts, you'll think of more ideas, and your children may come up with their own. Huzzah! You know your children, your community, your own strengths, and your family's resources better than anyone. These suggestions are meant to stimulate your creativity and to reassure you that it's never too soon to celebrate the seasons of life.

The Summer Sabbats for Infants
(Little ones younger than 1 year old)
Beltane

Ribbon mobiles over the bed, garlands of silk flowers (out of reach so Baby doesn't swallow them or choke), Summer scents (such as rose, jasmine, and freshly mown grass), laughter, plush robins and bluebirds, and musical toys. The idea here is to present the sounds, scents, and images of Beltane in comforting contexts. When it comes to perfumes or incense, don't make them too strong. Introduce them slowly to make sure Baby is not allergic! Chants can be lullabies, candles can light the room at feeding time, and incenses can go along with cuddling and gentle playing. Peekaboo can be played with decorative fans or silk bouquets. Dancing is fun, whether your baby is on the floor or a bench after a diaper change, or up in Mom's, Dad's, or Sibling's arms. (Don't toss babies—it literally rattles their brains. We used to think it was fun, and some babies enjoyed it, but now we know it's dangerous and best avoided.) Introduce Baby to bagpipes softly, and to bells and fiddles too. Babies love repetition, so folk songs with a lot of "um diddle-iddles" in them can inspire giggles and become favorites.

Litha

Babies like bright colors (even if parents like pastels), so a mobile made of small, colorful beach balls or glittery cardboard Suns will draw attention. All the sounds of Summer should be pleasant for Baby: Try CDs of surf, babbling brooks, and bird song if you can't be around the real thing. Babies love to watch older children at play too. As long as there's no risk of sunburn or insect bite (many sunscreens and insect repellents are too strong to use on babies), playing or napping on a blanket on the grass is great. Plush animals such as unicorns are also appropriate, and dragons are especially good at Litha. These plush toys should be small enough for Baby's wee fingers, and they should have no small bits that can be pulled off and swallowed or choked on.

Lammas

One of Baby's first solid foods is likely to be cereal made from grains or rice. This is perfect! (It is also fun to play in.) Some fruit juices can become part of Baby's diet now too—as any new food, they should be introduced one at a time and in small amounts to make sure your baby isn't allergic! The wicker texture of a cornucopia will intrigue exploring fingers and tongues, and may be a comfort to gums sprouting teeth. Again, outdoor play is lovely, so long as it's carefully supervised and properly shaded. Plush bees can be fun too—real ones, not so much! (We should teach our children caution, not fear, of bees. Stillness around bees is best learned as soon as possible, as the stereotypical "get it away" flailing about only alarms the bees and encourages them to sting in self-defense.) Babies quite naturally like to grab at things in the process of mastering both fine and gross motor skills—think of this as a harvest skill and work with it! As you can at Imbolc, teach Baby to associate gentle breezes and light rains with happy family moments.

Mabon

Even if Baby can't understand language yet, show off the beauty of Mabon's turning leaves—sound excited about it. Making sure not too many go in Baby's mouth, let Baby enjoy playing in piles of fallen leaves just like older kids do. Make an Autumn-leaf mobile with red, gold, and brown construction paper, to hang over Baby's crib. Decorate Baby's room with bouquets of Autumn leaves, wheat stalks, and dry flowers. Make Baby a corn-husk doll from craft materials or real corn cobs. (Pioneer and Native American babies played with these dolls, and they can make teething easier too.) The scents of apple pie and cinnamon can begin to delight Baby now, as they do everyone else. Baby may even be old enough to try a sip of apple cider—yum! (Do beware of too much sugar in any juices Baby enjoys.)

The Summer Sabbats for Early Childhood (Ages 1 – 5)

Beltane

Faces and flowers are among the first things children draw, and these are very appropriate for Beltane. Faces with flowers or in flowers can represent both the Goddess and the foliate aspect of the God, the Green Man. Children begin to understand the concept of costume when they are around 3 years old, so dressing up in festive garb for Beltane can be lots of fun. Decorate T-shirts with ribbons (make sure they're not long enough to trip on). Any kind of dancing is appropriate. Try music with a strong beat. Remember that some classical music inspires fluid move-ment, and some is nice to fall asleep to. Bells are another accessory of Beltane that little kids can enjoy, and with bells and tambourines, they can develop their sense of rhythm. Drums and xylophones are also fun musical toys. Circle dances are traditional for children, and the May dance is much more pleasant than "Ring Around the Rosie" (which actually refers to the effects of the bubonic plague)! Most kids love to twirl, and if they are on soft grass or carpet, they can dance around themselves as a pole!

Litha

You can teach young children "sunshine songs" such as "You Are My Sunshine." Even if you can't share the Summer pastimes you remember with your kids, you can probably come close with wading-pool parties and ice-cream socials, if nothing else. Some young children like to pre-tend to be superheroes. Maybe you can make your child a gold cape: It's something he or she can wear in the Litha Circle! If there are public gardens or arboretums where you live, organize a field trip and let your children appreciate the colors and scents of full Summer. Tending your own garden is something most kids will want to help you do too. Even playing in the dirt is fine; of course, making mud pies is something every child should have a chance to do. Children enjoy making paper flowers, and some can accordion-fold paper to make fans. You have to supervise their use of scissors and glue, but your own inner child will appreciate this extra playtime!

Lammas

Baking with little children takes a lot more time and involves a little more clean-up than it does for most adults, but it is well worth the extra time and effort. Just as fruit and veggies you harvest yourself taste bet-ter than ones you buy in the store, cookies and corn bread that you bake taste better than any you can buy from a comercial bakery. A carrot-shapped pan can be used to make corn bread, too, and even plain ol' corn bread can be decorated; dabs of frosting can be styled to look like kernels of corn! Strawberries are a traditional part of "first fruit" feasts, and they're easy for children to eat. In a Lammas Circle, a child can carry a bowl of straw-berries, offering them to everyone present as he or she enjoys them too. Four- or 5-year-olds can have fun on a berry-picking expedition. (If they are wearing old clothes, you won't have to worry about any stains. Scraps "dyed" with berry juice can be used in a Lammas quilt.)

Mabon

Let your toddlers and preschoolers roll in piles of Autumn leaves, supervised of course. If there are none where you live, cut some from construction paper and have your children toss them like confetti (just remember to "rake" them up from the lawn or living-room floor when you are done)! For some little children, popcorn is a delight. Who says popcorn strings are just for Yule? Also, in some places, it is chilly enough by Mabon to start using the fireplace. Four- and 5-year-olds can help carry kindling, and even younger children can help crumple paper to start the fire. Learning about fire this way helps teach young children the healthy respect for fire that they need to have. Can you hear and see flocks of migrating birds where you live? Point them out to your children. If you can, visit a local pond or lake and see if there are any ducks or geese left to feed, and explain that even if they fly away for the Winter, they will fly back in the Spring. Make an Autumn-colored foliate mask for your child to wear in the Mabon Circle.

The Summer Sabbats for Later Childhood (Ages 6–11)

Beltane

Use lightweight craft wire and nylon net or tulle to make fairy wings. Rather than paying close to $100 to buy a fairy bower from a catalog, use a large embroidery frame or metal hoop, a few yards of netting and ribbon, and some silk flowers to make your own. Hang your fairy bower from a porch beam or a tree limb, and put a child's table and chairs inside. Bake a cake and cut it into small squares and serve it with "fairy tea" (a mix of fruit juices, such as lemon, strawberry, or another favorite flavor). Encourage children to put on plays based on folktales; it will be even more fun if you help with the costumes. Beltane is a great time to learn how to braid—friendship bracelets are quite complex and better suited to an older child's dexterity, but simple hair braids are easy and fun. If you braid your child's hair while it's wet and let it dry before you unfasten the braid, it'll be festively wavy for your Beltane Circle. Bells and tambourines are just as much fun for older children as they are for younger ones. Some older children may be learning to play other instruments too. Music appreciation can be encouraged now. Let older children help you decide which tapes to play for the Maypole dance if you don't have a musician in your Circle.

Litha

Mid-Summer is a fine time to learn to recognize a few flowering plants and trees, and to learn about drying herbs. It's also a nice time to make daisy chains, and older children are usually dexterous enough to manage it. (All you have to do is make a small slit in the center of one daisy's stem, and slide the stem of another through it.) The chains can make great garlands for your hair or decorations for the altar and feast table. Older children can learn to make herbal teas, too, although at mid-Summer you'll probably want to drink them iced. "Sun tea" is fun to make during this season. (Put 4 or 5 tea bags in a jar and add a gallon of water. Leave it in the Sun for a few hours, and then enjoy! Sun tea can substitute for alcoholic Ale in your Litha Circle.) Making ice cream or "slushies" can be fun if you or someone you know has one of the machines to make it. Older children can gather rose petals from Litha to Lammas, and dry them in paper bags to use in potpourri next Winter.

Lammas

In addition to helping significantly with baking Cakes for the Lammas Circle, older children can be in charge of making something for the feast that follows your ritual. (See the section with Lammas activities for a recipe.) Older children can organize games, such as races and tugs-of-war (these can be played with non-Pagan children). For any child in school, basic research skills are useful, so sending them on a search for harvest traditions is appropriate. This may involve a trip to the library, or an hour or so on the computer. Nine-, 10-, and 11-year-olds could prepare short reports that would make dandy introductions to your Sabbat rites. Track how the Sun's position changes as the seasons progress by using a landmark in your yard or neighborhood.

Mabon

Provided with a cornucopia, older children can fill it with fruits and breads and offer it as an altar decoration. They can make altar cloths, too, decorating them with fabric paints or felt appliqués. Teach older children more of our chants: "Horned One" and "Hoof and Horn" are traditional among Wiccans for the harvest Sabbats. As well as learning the myths that explain seasonal changes, older children can understand how seasons occur in physical terms, how the Earth's rotation and orbit around the Sun affect how much sunlight falls on our landmasses, and the responses plants and animals have evolved to these changes. A walk through the woods to see what Autumn means to local plants and animals or a visit to a planetarium show would also be appropriate.

The Summer Sabbats for Adolescents (Ages 12–15)

Beltane

Adolescents are ready to understand Wicca's history and the longer history of Beltane as one of the original dividing points of the Year into two halves. The Maypole dance can be used as an illustration of various ethical points: personal responsibility (for one's own ribbon), cooperation (with other dancers and with the rhythm of the music), and so on. If a coming-of-age rite is appropriate, Beltane is an excellent time to schedule it.

Litha

How do other cultures celebrate the Sun's reaching its zenith? Adolescents can research this at the library or online. Recognizing that Litha is a celebration of confidence and abundance, kids these ages can come up with ways to share their own good fortune with others in their community, perhaps organizing a clothing or food drive. (Service agencies will tell you that poverty is year-round, even though we tend to be aware of other people's need only in the Winter months.) Adolescents who are interested in the Craft may also want to help you plan your Litha rite, or they may have a preference for the focus of the celebration.

Lammas

Did your children finish any Summer projects? Is there still time before school starts to complete them? Vacations may have been fun, but perhaps your kids learned something from their experiences. A collage of postcards or photographs might symbolically express new understandings that aren't so easily articulated in words. Has this Summer seen a first job, maybe yard work for neighbors, or help in a family business. That's an important milestone—a significant first harvest indeed.

Mabon

School has started now, and adolescents might be thinking about personal harvests in terms of study habits! Older adolescents may be thinking about college, or even careers, taking pride in the efforts they have already made toward such goals. It's certainly a good time to consider the consequences of their behavior and what changes need to be made before the final harvest celebration at Samhain. Mabon is an Equinox, like Ostara, and adolescents can learn the astronomical aspects of this Sabbat.

The Summer Sabbats for Young Adults (Ages 16 and older)

Beltane

At Beltane, as at Samhain, young adults can begin to study Jung and what other authors have to say about archetypes. They can also read other scholarly works about fairy lore. They can begin to consider the ways in which Wicca holds the Otherworld to be as real and important as our mundane realm. They can study other religions comparatively, too, and see how Wicca's understanding of the body as sacred may contradict the dominant paradigm. Some young adults are in love and may be planning weddings. Beltane is one of the most popular Sabbats for Wiccan handfastings, and even if a wedding is planned for another date, Beltane can help inspire the plans.

Litha

When Oak and Holly are about to trade reigns again, it seems like a good time for young adults to investigate the controversy about Wicca's history. Some insist that it is a holdover from traditions that predate the Inquisition, that 9 million proto-Wiccans were burned at the stake, and that a few covens actually survived in secrecy for 600 years or more. More recent and less emotionally invested scholarship makes it pretty clear that Wicca is a 20th-century construct, based on ancient ideals and related "poemogogically," as Starhawk might put it, to our Anglo-Celtic folk heritage. Young adults need to address the distinction between history and lore. While the Year is at its strongest and most outgoing is also a good time to consider Wiccan ethics, particularly those that inform spell-casting.

Lammas

Lammas is our first harvest festival, and one of our most precious harvests is our lore. Young adults can make themselves more familiar with the Anglo-Celtic stories that form part of Wicca's heritage. Lammas was one of the feasts at which tribal complaints were sorted out and laws were made and applied, so young adults can also think about the ways in which the Rede and the Law are illustrated in their personal stories. Lammas is a fine time for young adults to consider how the games of youth have strengthened—or distracted—them, and to recognize any patterns beginning to take shape in their Craft experience so far.

Mabon

Even before we've turned 16 or older, most of us have experienced some failures and losses; young adults can start to look at ways that they have turned—or can turn—losses into lessons and perceived weaknesses into strengths. At Mabon, the God dies in both His vegetable and animal forms, not only trusting rebirth in the Spring, but knowing that His life will sustain ours, and ours will embody His, through the Winter. Young adults can think about how their lives—even their "failures"—have helped and encouraged others, and how other people's work has influenced them. As at other Sabbats, young adults may be ready to write or perform significant parts of the Sabbat rite.

Appendix C

Correspondences

Virtually every "Wicca book" contains at least one table of correspondences; some feature several. Each Tradition of Wicca has developed its own correspondences, and there are differences among them. Some differences are slight, and some are major. There's no standard list of categories that every set of correspondences uses, which can be frustrating. Yet, because of Traditional variations, even when two different charts do share categories, their correspondences in those categories are probably not the same.

Usually the Directions, seasons, and times of day to which the Elements correspond and almost always the Sabbats to which they're connected are the same. But in other categories, there can be lots of differences. Many people new to the Craft take the first table of correspondences they read as gospel, and are shocked to find one offering different correlations. Others see right away that there are many different associations, and wonder how to tell which ones are the "right" ones.

Well, the "right" ones are the ones that make sense to you. Maybe it makes sense to you to use the same correspondences Gerald Gardner did, in which case you should rely on an authorized Gardnerian teacher. You won't find a full Gardnerian table of correspondences in print. They don't publish everything because they don't reveal their material except to their initiates. Much that you read about correspondences is derived from Gardnerian, but you won't be able to identify the differences unless you take the time and trouble to achieve a Gardnerian Initiation.

Maybe it makes sense to you to use another system, or maybe you'll find that portions of several charts are consistent with your way of thinking. Whatever correspondences you find effective in your work are fine to use as long you acknowledge your sources (keeping a bibliography in your *Book of Shadows* is helpful), you are consistent in using them, and as long as you don't pretend they're ancient or Traditional when they're not.

Speaking of consistency, there are some signs and symbols that are in use by most Wiccans, no matter what their Tradition. These are the "shorthand notation" symbols. (Most Traditions have a few of these symbols that they don't share, but there are some that are in common use.) I haven't included these "shorthand notation" symbols in the fairly conventional Table of Correspondences that follows, but I'll show you a few of them here:

△ signifies East and Air.

△ signifies South and Fire.

▽ signifies West and Water.

▽ signifies North and Earth.

⊙, ○, ⊖, and ⊕ are alternate Direction and Element signs.

♀ is commonly understood to mean "Goddess," and ♂ is used to mean "God.")O(and)●(signify the Triple Goddess.

These symbols are used mostly in ritual scripts or *Books of Shadows*, and sometimes used in spell-work; you won't find them substituting for words in a book like this. In other books, you may find different symbols that reflect other Traditions' correspondences or the author's personal system. I follow the Adventure Tradition, which has its own symbols, too, but I learned these from Gardnerian-trained and Alexandrian-trained Witches. (None of the symbols listed are available in any common fonts. The ones I've shown you are from Woolbats.)

The following chart is meant as a starting point for those new to the Craft who haven't yet developed their own sense of correspondence or who don't follow a Tradition that provides one. This chart, though it's not annotated or "explained," was developed with help from Rick Johnson, a British Traditional Priest in Tucson. He was my first teacher and offers the longest-running annual class in Arizona. He has volumes of notes and was kind enough to share several pages of correspondences with me for this book and its companion. His kindness extended even further: He gave me permission to make any changes I felt were appropriate.

I did make some, and so will you. Although the following correspondences make sense to me in terms of my experience and intuition, they may not "feel right" to you. This is not only okay, it's as it should be. When a different association makes more sense to you, I encourage you to change what you read in the chart. You should also add categories to your own chart, letting your research and practice of the Craft guide you. In the meantime, this chart is a place to begin, and also gives you a good example of what a correspondence chart looks like and how it works.

Other appropriate categories might include flowers, trees, musical instruments, and chants, for example. Some people find it a useful (and occasionally mirthful, which is also proper) exercise to add categories such as specific animal breeds (Siamese cats at East? Labrador retrievers at West?), academic disciplines, styles of poetry (Haiku at East? Free verse at West?), food groups, and so on. What make or model of car would you assign to each Quarter? What office equipment or article of clothing?

Do you think these exercises sound frivolous? Even if they do, they're good icebreakers for social events and good coven games; but they also deepen our understanding and support our efforts to think about the world in Wiccan terms. Our primary use of correspondences is to coordinate the elements (time, place, materials) of our magical workings, but they also help us relate various aspects of our lives, and help us see and work with the interconnections we hold holy. I've said it before and I'll say it again: It's not disrespectful to expand that understanding to the mundane world. I think we need to remember that even the seemingly most secular parts of our lives can be made sacred if we recognize their relationships to what's obviously holy.

You needn't feel limited by the form this chart takes, by the way. For instance, you can make your own chart in the form of a circle, dividing it into quarters, one for each season of the year, and organize your correspondences this way. After all, our calendar takes the form of a Wheel, and looking at our other associations that way can be helpful; "Seasons" is a category in most tables. The best perspective is always the one that lets you see the most connections, the correspondences, between your experience and that of others. In that sense, our correspondences are both a reason and a way to celebrate the seasons of life.

	Beltane	**Litha**	**Lammas**	**Mabon**
Activity	dancing Maypole	getting together	baking	wine-making
Animal(s)	goat; cat	horse; bee	rooster; pheasant	dog; wolf
Color(s)	bright: gold, red, pink, green	bright: gold, yellow, orange	dusky: gold, green, russet	dusky: orange, brown, violet, maroon
Direction	East (S.E.)	South	South (S.W.)	West
Element(s)	Air (Air & Fire)	Fire	Fire (Fire & Water)	Water
Elemental	Sylph	Salamander	Salamander	Undine
Gem(s)	emerald; rose quartz	diamond	peridot	amber; sapphire
Goddess	Blodeuwedd; Maeve	Brigid; Epona	Rhiannon	Modron
God	Green Man	Lugh	Dagda	Horned One; Mabon
Guardian Creature(s)	fairies	lizard; phoenix	gryphon	salmon
Inner focus	action; decision	nurture; love; sharing; honoring Gods	harvest; receiving	balance; thanks; acknowledgment
Metal(s)	silver; gold	gold	bronze	copper
Mythical Beast	unicorn	dragon	gryphon	minotaur
Season(s)	Spring/ Summer	Summer	Summer/ Autumn	Autumn
Time of Day	dawn	noon	noon	twilight
Tool	wand	sword	staff	altar

ibliography

Allen, Paula Gunn. *The Sacred Hoop: Recovering the Feminine in American Indian Traditions*. Boston: Beacon Press, 1986.

Aswynn, Freya. *Leaves of Yggdrasil: A Synthesis of Runes, Gods, Magic, Feminine Mysteries, and Folklore*. St. Paul, Minn.: Llewellyn, 1990.

Bosworth, Joseph and T. Northcote Toller, eds. *An Anglo-Saxon Dictionary*. London: Oxford University Press, 1898; rpt. 1964.

Bulfinch, Thomas. *Bulfinch's Mythology*. New York: Random House, Inc., 1993.

Carroll, Lewis. *Through the Looking-Glass* as presented in *The Complete Illustrated Lewis Carroll*. Hertfordshire, England: Wordsworth Editions, Ltd., 1996.

Chopra, Deepak. *Ageless Body, Timeless Mind: The Quantum Alternative to Growing Old*. New York: Harmony Books, 1993.

Cotterell, Arthur. *The Encyclopedia of Mythology*. London: Anness Publishing Limited, 1996.

Dillon, Myles, and Nora Chadwick. *The Celtic Realms: The History and the Culture of the Celtic Peoples From Pre-History to the Norman Invasion*. Edison, N.J.: Castle Books, 2003.

Eliade, Mircea. *Patterns in Comparative Religion*. Lincoln, Nebr.: University of Nebraska Press, 1996.

Farrar, Janet, and Stewart Farrar. *A Witches Bible Compleat*. New York: Magickal Childe, Inc. 1984.

Franklin, Anna. *Midsummer: Magical Celebrations of the Summer Solstice*. St. Paul, Minn.: Llewellyn Publications, 2002.

Franklin, Anna and Paul Mason. *Lammas: Celebrating the Fruits of the First Harvest*. St. Paul, Minn.: Llewellyn Publications, 2001.

Friend, Hilderic. *Flowers and Flower Lore*. New York: John B. Alden, Publisher, 1889.

Gamlinginn. "Concerning the Modern Asatru Calendar" (unpublished article). Silver City, N. Mex.: 2003.

Grimassi, Raven. *Beltane: Springtime Rituals, Lore & Celebration*. St. Paul, Minn.: Llewellyn Publications, 2001.

Gundarsson, Kveldulf. *Teutonic Magic: The Magical and Spiritual Practices of the Germanic People*. St. Paul, Minn.: Llewellyn Publications, 1990.

Hutton, Ronald. *The Rise and Fall of Merry England: The Ritual Year 1400–1700*. New York: Oxford University Press, 1994.

———. *The Stations of the Sun*. New York: Oxford University Press, 1996.

———. *The Triumph of the Moon: A History of Modern Pagan Witchcraft*. New York: Oxford University Press, 1999.

Johnson, Rick. *Sabbat Correspondences* (N.P., 1980–2000).

MacCana, Proinsias. *Celtic Mythology*. London: Hamlyn Publishing Group, 1970.

MacCulloch, J.A., *The Religion of the Ancient Celts*. London: Constable and Company, Ltd., 1991.

Madden, Kristin. *Mabon: Celebrating the Autumn Equinox*. St. Paul, Minn.: Llewellyn Publications, 2002.

Nelson, Chandra. "May Dew Alternatives." *Tapestry*, 2004 Ostara/Beltane issue.

O'Gaea, Ashleen. *Celebrating the Seasons of Life: Samhain to Ostara*. Franklin Lakes, N.J.: New Page Books, 2004.

———. *Raising Witches*. Franklin Lakes, N.J.: New Page Books, 2002.

Riccio, Dolores. *Superfoods: 300 Recipes for Foods That Heal Body and Mind*. New York: Warner Books, 1992.

Shakespeare, William. *A Midsummer Night's Dream*. Mineola, N.Y.: Dover Publications, 2003.

Thomas, Kirk. E-mails to author, 2003.

Tolkien, J.R.R. *The Fellowship of the Ring*. New York: Ballantine Books, 1965.

Weil, Dr. Andrew. *Eating Well for Optimum Health*. New York: Alfred A. Knopf, 2000.

ndex

About the Author

ASHLEEN O'GAEA is the author of several books about Wicca, including *Raising Witches: Teaching the Wiccan Faith to Children* (New Page Books, 2002). She and her husband/Priest Canyondancer were among the founders, and are Board Members Emeritus of the Tucson Area Wiccan-Pagan Network (T.A.W.N.), and, while leading Campsight Coven for 13 years, developed and articulated the Adventure Tradition of Wicca. O'Gaea is a founding Board member and the senior corresponding Priestess for Mother Earth Ministries-ATC, a Neo-Pagan prison ministry based in Tucson, Arizona. She and Canyondancer offer presentations about various aspects of Wicca and share their home with a loveable Aussie-Chow-Idiot mix and three young, affectionate cats.

CPSIA information can be obtained at www.ICGtesting.com

260076BV00001B/27/P

9 781564 147325